To the Irish Housewives and all the women with whom
I have worked, who have given me so much.
This is your story as I see it.

Acknowledgements

First of all my thanks to Mary Cullen who inspired me to write this book; her help, advice and encouragement also ensured that I completed the task. To Rosemary Cullen Owens for providing instant help with historical information on several occasions. To Dr Margaret MacCurtain for her friendship and belief in my ability to undertake this book. To Nuala Fennell, TD, for her help with the section on the Irish Women's Liberation Movement. To Daisy Swanton for information about her mother, Lucy Kingston. To Andrée Sheehy Skeffington, to whom I and the Housewives owe so much, for her help and advice with the first part of the book. To Nora F Browne and Kathleen Delap who read and 'passed' the section on the ad-hoc committee and the Council for the Status of Women. Special thanks to Gretta Morrison who generously gave her time to read through IHA reports and help with the research. My gratitude to all the Housewives and friends, too numerous to mention, who have helped through lending me photographs and documents, and taken over tasks to give me time to write 'the book'.

To Attic Press who agreed to publish the book, Róisín Conroy and Ailbhe Smyth for their encouragement, and Gráinne Healy, the managing editor, for her skill and advice - and patience with missed deadlines. My thanks to Georgie Grey, Gretta Morrison and Geraldine Watts for helping to read and proof the text with me. To Paul Schmitz who initiated me into the mysteries of the word processor with great patience and who appeared like magic when technical problems arose. Last, but not least to my husband, Robert, who bore with me and sustained me throughout the somewhat turbulent gestation of this book. He believes that he started the IHA when he said to me, 'It's no use complaining to me about things that are wrong! Go away and talk to somebody who can change them'!

Contents

Foreword

Hilda Tweedy is one of a group in twentieth-century Ireland whose firm grasp of the idiom of everyday life has enabled them to diagnose the patient's condition with unerring accuracy, and prescribe the cure. A founder-member of the Irish Housewives Association which is the subject of her reflective study, in 1942 she and her co-founders were a significant minority who developed for women in Ireland the real meaning of citizenship. The Irish Free State had, by then, become a state where gendered political forces had limited women's access to political and economic power. It was a critical time for the citizens of the Irish Free State. Removed from the theatre of the European war by its constitutional stand on neutrality, the state paid the price in scarcity of money, food and fuel. There was stark poverty in many households and the spectre of tuberculosis struck with deadly effect at families. Children suffered woeful malnutrition with little hope of medical alleviation.

Hilda Tweedy who had returned from a teaching life in Egypt in 1936 wanted to change that scenario. For her it was not a simple recipe of applying sporadic remedies of 'food-drops', rather it was a searching out of strategies to influence government policy to take requisite action. Of Hilda Tweedy it can be said that she possessed a capacity, not once but several times in her life for discerning that a time had come when one of her ideas was unstoppable. With a small circle of like-minded women, Andrée Sheehy Skeffington, Marguerite Skelton, Sheila Mallagh and Nancye Simmons in 1941 they formed a pressure group and drew up a petition dubbed 'the housewives petition' and sent copies of it to every member of Dáil Eireann before Budget Day demanding fair prices for producer and consumer and equitable distribution of goods, including food. So government rationing and the book of coupons were introduced, a familiar routine of the Irish citizen's life in the forties. Less than a year later Hilda Tweedy, Andrée Sheehy Skeffington,

Susan Manning and Louie Bennett convened the first meeting of the Irish Housewives Association. Over a sustained period of time it has been one of the most influential voices in consumer affairs, monitoring price-controls, lobbying successive governments, and teaching women to play an active role in community affairs as they impinged on economic policy. The Irish Housewives Association while not aligning itself with any particular political party encouraged women to run for office at a period when women's entry into the public sphere had been sharply curtailed.

Sturdily year after year the Association took on the politico-economic establishment confounding their opponents by seeming to glory in their own self-styled appellation 'Irish housewife'. Reproached for their campaign on school meals, Hilda Tweedy recalls one Reverend gentleman who said ' we would be breaking up the sanctity of the home if children were to be fed at school.' Hilda was among those who supported the Minister for Health, Dr Noel Browne in the Mother and Child Scheme. She remembers with amusement a public meeting when her contribution was drowned by an audience who struck up 'Faith of Our Fathers'. Despite rumours that it was pink the Irish Housewives Association with its energetic executive, (Hilda was joint secretary for years and then chairperson, and later still treasurer) developed a solidarity with women's organisations country-wide, forming coalitions that worked as a pressure group if an issue concerning consumer problems arose. Drawing upon remembered tactics which had been used earlier in the suffrage campaigns such as deputations to cabinet ministers, submitting evidence to Dáil committees, writing to county and city councillors as well as feeding the newspapers with their own press-statements, they showed a shrewd sense of where to lean as a lobby. Conscious of the dual role of women in the mid-century they presented to the public the solid frontage of the Irish housewife; strategically they instructed their members on how to negotiate the complex maze of the Irish party machinery.

Some years after stating their aims, the Housewives incorporated the Irish Women's Citizen Association into their membership thus linking with the older Suffrage Society of

8

1874, which in 1915 had become the Suffrage and Local Government Association. Hilda Tweedy is justly proud of the continuity between the older radical stream of feminism with the concerns of the new Ireland after the post-war years. How they won recognition from the Trade Union Congress and received affiliation with the International Alliance of Women is part of the story that Hilda Tweedy unfolds in her account. From early on she had perceived the importance of attending international conferences and between 1946 and 1986 she represented the Irish Housewives Association so many times at the International Alliance of Women, where she became an important member of the executive, that she truly was one of the best unofficial diplomats Ireland possessed. In writing the history of the association she served so magnificently, Hilda Tweedy has brought to light what has remained invisible to leading historians: women's ability to intervene in state policy around price control, and the socialisation of housework in the eyes of the public and the media. Previously in 1931 the Joint Committee of Women's Societies and Social Workers was formed to process issues dealing with social policy and legislation, and the Irish Housewives Association affiliated to that body realising that the sharing of information and experience contributed to the effectiveness of the objective. The Irish Housewives Association supported the Irish Women Laundry Workers' Strike in 1945 which resulted in state recognition of a fortnight's holidays in the year. They taught the 'housewife' to claim her rights, and if she was a member of the Irish Countrywomen's association, or later in the fifties a member of the Business and Professional Women's Association, then the more powerful the lobby. The coalitions of interest that women developed in the middle decades of the twentieth century prepared the climate for establishing the Council for the Status of Women of which Hilda Tweedy was chairwoman, first of the ad hoc committee, 1968-70, and when the Council for the Status of Women was set up she was elected its first chairwoman 1972-78.

She laughs when she is described as a 'redoubtable old-style feminist'. She comes from a minority which has played a significant role in defining the nature of Irish Feminism. Born in

Clones, county Monaghan, she spent her childhood in Athlone where her father was the Church of Ireland rector. Twice in her life she passed through the classrooms of Alexandra College Dublin, first as pupil and later as teacher - mathematics was her strong interest. Marriage to Robert Tweedy in 1936 brought her back to Dublin and though their three adult children live in different parts of the world, home remains the house and garden in Stillorgan. Conferred with the degree of Doctor in Laws, honoris causa, by Trinity College Dublin in 1990, it was proper that the citation should list among Hilda Anderson Tweedy's achievements her remarkable steadfastness in working to improve the status of women and her work as co-founder and active member of the Irish Housewives Association.

Margaret Mac Curtain,
History Department,
University College Dublin

Beginnings

Cast your mind back to 1941. This was the time of the 'Emergency'. The Second World War was at its height and Ireland, as a neutral country, was suffering shortages of all imported goods. Those who had money were buying sacks of sugar and flour, and chests of tea. The rest managed as best they could. There was no rationing, prices soared and scarce goods disappeared under the counter. There was real poverty and malnutrition and children in particular suffered a lot.

These conditions were highlighted in the spring of 1941 when Dr Robert Collis, the well-known Dublin paediatrician, initiated the Marrowbone Lane Fund to help children when they came out of hospital, so that they should not return to the poor conditions which had caused their illnesses in the first case. The role of the Fund was to provide nutritious food and improve housing conditions.

At the same time Judge Wyllie and a group of supporters opened non-profit-making restaurants called 'Goodwill Restaurants' which provided simple nourishing meals at a low cost. Social welfare provisions were then quite inadequate to deal with the 'Emergency' problems. There were no services such as school meals, or meals on wheels. The old, children and the unemployed suffered particularly. Other efforts to improve conditions were made by the Mount Street Club, which was initiated by Paddy Somerville Large and a group of friends and run as a co-operative for unemployed men. This organisation provided workshops for craftwork and plots of land to grow vegetables and fruit. Householders who had gardens grew produce to supplement their diet as imported fruit and vegetables were non-existent.

For some time I had been aware of the hard conditions of the people and wanted to do something to help. So in February 1941 I made a list of friends whom I thought would be interested and wrote a letter to them beginning `What does Marrowbone Lane mean to you?' I invited them to my home in Stillorgan to discuss what could be done. I had divided the women into groups of five or six. The night before the first group was due to arrive I became nervous about the whole project. I wondered what I really hoped to achieve: I did not want just another organisation to alleviate conditions on the surface, but rather to get to the root of the matter, to attack the causes of such hardship. Andrée Sheehy Skeffington's name was on the list. I had been holding her for a future date. But that night, as I thought things over, I realised that she was the one person on my list who had the experience and the political know-how to shape my rather nebulous idea into a working project. I phoned Andrée and explained my dilemma and asked her to leave whatever she was doing the following afternoon and come to the first gathering. This she agreed to do.

Five women met at that first meeting: Andrée Sheehy Skeffington, Marguerite Skelton, Nancye Simmons, Sheila Mallagh and myself. Who were these women? Andrée Skeffington, (née Denis), was born in Amiens, graduated from the Sorbonne, and spent a year in the USA on a scholarship. She met Owen Sheehy Skeffington in 1928 when he spent a summer with the Denis family, Madame Denis having been a friend of the Sheehy family. Andrée and Owen were married in 1935 and Andrée came to live in Dublin. Owen was at that time a lecturer in French in Trinity College, while Andrée did translations and private classes in French.

Marguerite Skelton belonged to the well-known Quaker family, the Jacobs of Waterford. She was educated at a Quaker school in England after which she studied Social Science. Before her marriage to Jack Skelton, who worked in insurance, in 1938, she worked in the welfare department of W R Jacob and Co.

Sheila Mallagh also belonged to the Society of Friends. Her name was Sheila Webb before her marriage to Terence Mallagh, a civil engineer. She was always interested in the welfare of prisoners and was a prison visitor to Mountjoy. She taught ballroom dancing for several years.

Nancye Simmons (née James), was educated at Alexandra School after which she did a secretarial course at Miss Galway's

Secretarial College. She worked with the British Reinforced Concrete Engineering Company, a job she kept for a while after her marriage to Eric Simmons, a teacher at Mountjoy School. She also worked from time to time at Mercer's Hospital, doing secretarial work or acting as almoner when required. Nancye was always interested in the Women's Missionary Society of the Presbyterian Church.

The fifth member of the group, myself, had been educated at Alexandra School and College. In 1929 I joined my parents in Alexandria, Egypt, where my father was Rector of St Mark's Church. I started a small school on PNEU methods for English speaking children while working for a Maths degree at London University as an extern student. I married Robert Tweedy, the manager of the Court Laundry, Harcourt Street, Dublin, and came back to live in Ireland in 1936, dropping out of my Maths course.

In 1941 we were all young married women, in our late twenties or early thirties. Marguerite, Sheila and I had one child each. Andrée and Nancye had not started their families yet. Our husbands earned between four and eight pounds per week at that time, so we could not be described as well-off, although the value of money was quite different then. It was unusual for married women to work outside the home and quite difficult for them to find jobs. I applied to teach twelve-year old girls, but was turned down because I was a married woman and was told, 'It would not be nice for the girls if you became pregnant' !

So we met that afternoon in 1941 and discussed what we could do to better conditions in the Ireland of the 'Emergency'. We had a long discussion, each person adding to the list of what had to be done. Andrée suggested that we should draw up a petition to the government and get women who were interested to sign it.

It was agreed to speak to groups of women, getting as many signatures as possible before Budget Day, 5 May 1941. The final wording of the petition was agreed and we decided to send it, signed by fifty-one women, to the government, the opposition parties and the press the day before the budget. On the Sunday before the budget, Andrée and her husband, Owen, came to my home and we worked all day typing the petition, (three copies at a time on an ancient portable type-writer. No word-processors or photo-copying machines then!) Andrée and I took turns at the typing, with Owen relieving us at times.

The petition caught the imagination of the press and we got coverage from the national papers under the heading 'Housewives Petition'. It dealt with the production and distribution of food, advocating fair prices for producer and consumer, and suggesting ways in which the farmer could be encouraged to produce more, including compulsory tillage of forty per cent of all arable land, credit facilities at a lower rate of two per cent, free lease of extra machinery and a government guarantee of fair prices to farmers so that they could maintain a decent standard of living, employ more labour on the land and pay standard wages to employees.

The petition asked for national registration of all essential foodstuffs and immediate and effective rationing where there was a present, or possible, shortage, to sell at a standard price within reach of all. We called for a government fruit and vegetable market to supply retailers and control retail prices. The production and distribution of fuel was also dealt with. An intensive turf-cutting campaign was advocated, so too was protection against the cutting of trees, control of the consumption of gas and electricity, the control of the distribution and the price of coal. We also called for prohibition of the use of coal as fuel for pleasure cars.

We looked for special measures to ensure that the poor and unemployed would be safeguarded against the rise in the cost of living, measures such as a proportional increase in unemployment allowance, a free milk scheme for nursing and expectant mothers and the raising of the age from five to eight years of children of the unemployed eligible for the free milk scheme. We urged the government to organise a comprehensive plan embracing all existing schemes for communal feeding centres, including cooking centres and mobile kitchens.

We continued to collect signatures for our petition and send them to the government. Eventually 640 women signed. It is interesting to recall the reasons women gave for not signing. 'My husband would not like me to sign anything,' said one. 'I would be afraid to sign because if the Nazis get here they would immediately imprison anyone who was an agitator,' replied another.

Louie Bennett and her sister, Susan Manning, had been early signatories of the petition at one of Andrée's groups and in 1942 they contacted Andrée and me, saying it was a pity to waste the momentum generated by the petition and suggesting that an organisation should be formed to carry on the work. Louie Bennett, chief executive of the Irish Women Workers Union, offered their hall as the venue for our meeting. We notified the 640 signatories, naïvely wondering if the hall would be large enough to hold them. We need not have worried. Forty turned up and twelve stayed to form the Irish Housewives Committee on 12 May 1942.

Our first meeting was held in the Friends Meeting House in Eustace Street. We decided to call ourselves the Irish Housewives Committee to capitalise on the name 'Housewives' which had been given to us by the press when the petition was sent to the government.

Susan Manning was elected 'chairman', (those were the days before the term `chairwoman' or `chairperson' was adopted by any women's group in Ireland; that came later in the '70s). Betty Morrissey was elected honorary treasurer and Andrée Skeffington and myself joint honorary secretaries. The Committee was to be non-party and non-sectarian. Women of all political parties, and none, women from the different churches, as well as those with no sectarian commitments, joined. At first the membership was predominantly Protestant, but over the years adjusted to proportional representation of the various churches. Unfortunately the IHA, (as it is now known), never attracted the number of women living in working class districts which we would have liked. Early membership was recruited amongst friends. They organised groups in their own homes to hear members of the IHA speak of our work, so new members tended to be from the same background. Later we organised meetings in different districts, but never really succeeded in ridding ourselves of a middle-class image. This has been a weakness in the IHA, but the '40s were a survival period. Most women had neither the time nor the money to attend meetings, and were occupied solely with the mechanics of living.

The minimum subscription to the IHA was fixed at one shilling in order to put membership within reach of as many women as possible. The ensuing amount from subscriptions was inadequate for our needs. It was due to the generosity of Mr Carr Lett, the husband of one of our members, Beryl Carr Lett, who lent us his legal rooms at 16 St Stephen's Green, that we were able to survive our first year. The hard work and enthusiasm of our members cut down expenses to a minimum. They walked or cycled round Dublin and the suburbs, delivering letters to save postage.

Money has always been a problem for the IHA as we have never had funding from any source, relying entirely on the subscriptions of members and money they have raised by running sales or social functions. The government has, on occasion, given grants, mostly in the form of air fares, to enable a member to attend meetings connected with consumer affairs. Lack of money prevented us from having premises of our own, and forced us to dissipate our energies raising money when we could have been doing more important work.

On formation, four points were chosen from the petition as a basis for our work: price control and rationing, transport, school meals, and salvage of waste. Our method of work was to investigate fully the subject in hand, eg the price of meat from the sale of cattle in the market, through the abattoir to the wholesaler, to the cutting up of the carcass by the retailer. When sure of our facts we wrote letters to the government and the press, lobbied TDs and senators, and approached state and semi-state bodies, as well as professional and trade bodies and voluntary organisations for information and support. Though small in number we quickly built up a reputation for reliability and tenacity of purpose. It was amusing to hear recently from reliable sources that during Mr de Valera's term as Taoiseach it was the duty of one of his senior staff to keep a file on the newspaper reports of the doings of the Irish Housewives !

During our first year we were greatly concerned with the

price and distribution of goods. We believed that all essential commodities should be rationed before a shortage occurred and the price strictly controlled. We pressed for a special rationing scheme for children, to ensure they got preferential treatment in the distribution of citrus fruits, cereals, sugar and fresh TT (tuberculin tested) milk, at special prices where necessary, and asked for cheap cod-liver oil for children during the winter.

We campaigned for school meals, asking for a hot meal and one third of a pint of milk daily for each child. We also asked for a pint of TT milk daily for pregnant women, nursing mothers and children under five at a special price of two old pence per pint. The IHA organised a march through the streets of Dublin highlighting children's special needs, carrying posters with slogans such as 'The Children must be Fed', 'War on TB', 'Pure Milk', 'Clean Food', 'Fair Prices', 'Open the Municipal Kitchens', 'Give the Children Dinner and not Bread'. During the course of this campaign we lobbied doctors, schools, TDs and members of Dublin Corporation. When putting our case to the Schools Committee of the Corporation one Reverend gentleman said that we would be breaking up the sanctity of the home if children were fed at school! Over the years we have come up against some extraordinary attitudes to what we considered common sense suggestions.

In our investigations we studied the activities of the Pigs and Bacon Marketing Boards and the Dublin and Cork District Milk Boards. We were disappointed to find these boards were mostly concerned with the interests of the middlemen and distributors rather than the producer and the consumer. This led us to study the supply and quality of milk which eventually led to the Milk Tribunal at which we gave evidence in 1945.

Much of our initial work led to on-going campaigns such as the campaigns for safer milk, the salvage of waste, and improvements in transport. How many people know that the IHA were the first to press for free transport for pensioners? That first year set the pattern for our work and great credit must go to Andrée Skeffington who trained us in research. At the end of 1945 our membership had risen to seventy-seven and our name was known.

At the beginning the Housewives managed to get along without a constitution, but as numbers grew this became necessary. In 1946 we changed the name to the Irish Housewives Association (IHA), and much thought was given to stating our objectives. From the beginning we had been non-party and non-sectarian. We decided on the following: (a) To unite housewives so that they shall recognise, and gain recognition for, their right to play an active part in all spheres of planning for the community; (b) To secure all such reforms as are necessary to establish a real equality of liberties, status and opportunity for all persons; (c) The aims and general policy shall be to defend consumers' rights as they are affected by supply, distribution and price of essential commodities, to suggest legislation or take practical steps to safeguard their interests, as well as generally to deal with matters affecting the home; (d) To take steps to defend consumers against all taxation on necessary food, fuel and clothing.

Membership was open to all women who accepted the constitution. Men could become associate members, but they had no vote and were not eligible for office. We have never had more than half a dozen male members in all our fifty years, but we must pay tribute to the many men who have helped us, not forgetting the husbands whose co-operation in the home made it possible to carry out our work.

When the IHA was founded in 1942 there were several women's organisations in Ireland working to improve the place of women in our society. A number of these had been part of the suffrage movement. The main women's organisations functioning at the time of the foundation of the IHA were as follows:

The Irish Countrywomen's Association (ICA), was founded in 1910 as the United Irishwomen, an organisation which arose from the Irish Co-operative movement, through Horace Plunkett who felt that women should be responsible for the 'Better Living' part of the co-operative slogan, 'Better Business - Better Living'. In 1934 the United Irishwomen changed their name to the Irish Countrywomen's Association with a new constitution and the specific aim of improving conditions for women living in rural

Ireland and of encouraging rural crafts. As physical conditions improved they sought to raise awareness and encourage all women to play an active part in their community. Muriel Gahan,(now Dr Muriel Gahan and still very active in the ICA), who managed the Country Shop which was set up to sell craftwork and country produce and also became a very popular restaurant, provided a room at the Country Shop free, or at a nominal fee, when the IHA needed a venue for public meetings and was struggling for financial survival. Down the years we have considered the ICA as a sister organisation, and we have supported each other on various issues.

The Irish Women Workers Union (IWWU), was founded in 1911 and re-organised by Louie Bennett in 1916. It organised the women in the printing trade, and later, women in the laundry industry. We worked closely with Louie Bennett, joining a march organised by IWWU to protest against the lack of effective price control while wages were stabilised. The IHA was also involved with her in preparing a charter to improve the lot of women in domestic service, women who were greatly exploited by those who employed them.

The Irish Women Citizens Association was formed in 1923 to carry on the work of the Irish Women's Suffrage and Local Government Association. The history of this Association is dealt with in detail later as it was incorporated in the IHA in 1948.

In 1937 when Eamonn de Valera introduced the present Constitution, Hanna Sheehy Skeffington and a group of women, including members of the Women Graduates Association and the Irish Women Citizens Association, protested against the curtailment of freedom for women contained in the section of the Irish Constitution on the family, virtually confining women to the home. The group sent postcards to the electorate, particularly to women, saying 'Vote No to the Constitution'. The Constitution was passed and the results, as predicted, are still with us today. After the referendum Hanna Sheehy Skeffington contemplated the formation of a women's political party, but instead the Women's Social and Political League was founded, with Hanna in the chair, to monitor legislation affecting women. Hanna Sheehy Skeffington was a good friend to the IHA and we

19

benefitted from her advice and experience in our formative period. When, in 1943, the League put Hanna forward as an Independent candidate for the Dáil, the IHA enthusiastically endorsed her candidature.

The Joint Committee of Women's Societies and Social Workers was set up in 1931 when the Corrigan Report on Sexual Offences was presented to the then Fine Gael government, and the suggestions of social workers were rejected. These suggestions related to issues such as : raising the age of consent to eighteen years; equal treatment in law for a woman found soliciting and her client; provision of a women's police force; appointment of more women probation officers; jury service for women on the same terms as men. In 1942 the following organisations were affiliated to the 'Joint Committee':

Central Association of Irish School Mistresses, Dublin Hospital Almoners Association, Irish Matrons Association, Irish Women Citizens Association, Women's National Health Association, Women's Social and Progressive League, Women Graduates Association of Trinity College, Women Graduates Association of National University, Girls Friendly Society, Saor an Leanbh, Irish Nurses Association, St Patrick's Guild, Mothers Union, Irish Women Workers Union.

The IHA joined the 'Joint Committee' in 1946 when the main issues were: boarded-out children, legal adoption and prison reform. We have worked closely with the Joint Committee ever since on various issues concerning the welfare of women and children and the community at large. On several occasions the IHA representative has been elected to the chair of the Joint Committee.

The Dublin Club of the Soroptimists International was founded in 1938 by Professor Agnes Farrelly. It is a service club and works to improve social conditions for the under-privileged, and as such has always been interested in the status of women.

The IHA worked with the existing organisations and in 1943 became affiliated to the Women's Emergency Conference which had been formed from the representatives of existing organisations under the chair of Mrs Neill Watson of the Methodist Women's Committee; its task was to deal with war conditions, particularly those affecting children and the least privileged. We helped in their surveys of shortages and our delegates took part in an inquiry into the potato supply. The Emergency Conference worked on until 1946 when it was felt to be redundant after the war ended.

Feminist issues

The Irish Housewives always had an interest in feminist issues. We learned that making pleas to the government was not enough. We needed committed women in political life, women in the places where the decisions were being made. During our first year we endorsed the candidature of Hanna Sheehy Skeffington as an Independent candidate for the Dáil but unfortunately she was not elected. At that time the women TDs were usually widows, put there by political parties on the death of their husbands to secure the seat on a sympathy vote. Little was heard from them, or of them. We called them the 'silent sisters', but perhaps that was a hasty judgement. They probably proved their worth on the various committees then deemed suitable for women, but their work was not reported.

In November 1947 the Irish Women Citizens Association was incorporated into the IHA and a further clause was added to the objectives of the Association: (e) To carry on the work of the Irish Women Citizens Association (incorporated 1947), with affiliation to the International Alliance of Women (IAW), through the international committee of the Irish Housewives Association. The IHA has always been proud of the link with the 'Women Citizens' and of the confidence they displayed in our ability to carry on their important work.

The Irish Women Citizens Association (name changed circa 1919), which grew out of the IWSLGA (founded 1874), had worked to educate and encourage women in the use of the vote which they had obtained at the initiation of the state in 1922. The Citizens felt they had attained their objective. They were not gaining new members and numbers were dwindling, so they asked the IHA if they could join the Association as a group and the international committee of the IHA was formed with their secretary, Lucy Kingston, as its secretary, and our members who were interested in international affairs and women's rights joined this committee.

The IHA benefitted greatly by this amalgamation of interests and not least from the new members it gained, amongst whom were Connie Allen, Mrs Clifton, Mrs Jean Coote, later chairwoman of the IHA, Miss Rosamund Jacob, Mrs Kyle, Miss Ella Mills, Mrs Murphy and Mrs Lucy Kingston. Susan Manning and her sister, Louie Bennett, also belonged to the Women Citizens, but with Connie Allen, were already founding members of the IHA. These were all interesting women with great experience of working for women's rights.

Lucy Kingston was remarkable and the IHA was fortunate to have a woman of her calibre and experience to help us in our formative years. She worked in various capacities on the international committee and on the central committee of the IHA until her death in 1969. Lucy Kingston (née Lawrenson), was a woman with considerable personal charm and a gentle quiet manner who could speak with great force and conviction on issues dear to her. Born in 1892, she was a keen pacificist and feminist all her life. From 1912 onwards she belonged to the following organisations: The Irish Women's Suffrage Federation, Irish Women's Reform League, Irish Women's Franchise League, Irish Women's international League, later to become the Women's International League for Peace and Freedom (WILPF). (The Irish branch of WILPF declined during the Second World War and finally closed down, though women such as Lucy Kingston and Louie Bennett remained as individual members. In 1991 an Irish Branch of WILPF was re-established by a group of women motivated by their desire to work for peace at the time of the Gulf War, amongst whom was the historian Rosemary Cullen Owens). In 1914 Lucy married Samuel Kingston. They had three children but Lucy continued with her interests. In the 1920s she joined the Quakers and worked with them and other groups in the 1930s assisting refugees from Hitler's Germany. When war broke out she and her husband helped these refugees to gain work permits in Ireland. During this period Lucy was very active in the Women's Social and Progressive League, the National Council of Women, (neither of which survived the Emergency period), and the Irish Women Citizens Association.

Another benefit from the incorporation of the Irish Women

Citizens was a legacy from the estate of Rebecca Wilson. She had bequeathed a sum of money to the Irish Women's Suffrage League and it was decided by the court that the IHA was the direct successor to the Irish Women's Suffrage League, through the Irish Women Citizen's Association. The IHA has always been grateful to Lucy Kingston who gave evidence to prove that the IHA was the rightful successor and thus secured this legacy; though a small sum, it helped us to put our finances on a firmer basis.

The amalgamation with the Irish Women Citizens brought a new dimension into the IHA through its affiliation to the International Alliance of Women (IAW). Until 1948 we had been very busy with domestic issues, and indeed many Irish women felt that there was so much to be done at home we should not get involved abroad. This was an attitude that kept cropping up in women's groups until the 1970s when the United Nations designated 1975 as UN International Women's Year with the UN World Conference in Mexico which focused attention on the status of women all over the world. Women then realised the importance of the exchange of ideas and experiences, and networking began.

The affiliation to the International Alliance of Women opened new doors for us and strengthened our feminist convictions. The IAW started in the USA in 1902 when Elizabeth Stanton, Carrie Chapman Catt and Susan B Anthony organised an International Woman Suffrage Conference as part of the annual convention of the National American Woman Suffrage Association, which was attended by delegates from ten countries. In 1904 a second meeting of the International Woman Suffrage Conference was held in Berlin and adopted the following charter:

(1) That men and women are born equally free and independent members of the human race; equally endowed with intelligence and ability, and equally entitled to the free exercise of their individual rights and liberty.

(2) That the natural relation of the sexes is that of interdependence and co-operation, and that the repression of the rights and liberty of one sex inevitably works injury to the other,

and hence to the whole race.

(3) That in all lands, those laws, creeds and customs which have tended to restrict women to a position of dependence, to discourage their education, to impede the development of their natural gifts, and to subordinate their individuality, have been based on false theories, and have produced an artificial and unjust relation to the sexes in modern society.

(4) That self-government in the home and the state is the inalienable right of every normal adult, and the refusal of this right to women has resulted in social, legal and economic injustice to them, and has also intensified the existing economic disturbances throughout the world.

(5) That governments which impose taxes and laws upon their women citizens without giving them the right of consent or dissent, which is granted to men citizens, exercise a tyranny inconsistent with just government.

(6) That the ballot is the only legal and permanent means of defending the rights to the 'life, liberty and the pursuit of happiness', pronounced inalienable by the American Declaration of Independence, and accepted as inalienable by all civilised nations. In any representative form of government, therefore, women should be vested with all political rights and privileges of electors. (See *Woman into Citizen*, by Arnold Whittick, 1979.)

The agreed object of IAW was 'to secure the enfranchisement of the women of all nations, and to unite the friends of women suffrage throughout the world in organised co-operation and fraternal helpfulness'. (It was a long time before feminists became conscious of the implications of using male terminology!)

In July 1914 the International Woman Suffrage Alliance delivered a manifesto to the Foreign Office and all the foreign embassies in London, calling upon governments to avert the threatened war and pointing out that women had no direct power to control whether they lived in peace or at war.

At the Peace Conference held in Paris in January 1919 there was no representation of women, or women's interests, so the Union Francaise pour le Suffrage des Femmes invited delegates from the Allied countries affiliated to the International Woman

Suffrage Alliance (to become International Alliance of Women (IAW) in 1926), to a conference in Paris to obtain consideration of the position of women in the world and to seek representation of women at the Peace Conference. Millicent Fawcett, one of the delegates from Britain, as spokeswoman, asked President Wilson for his approval of representation of women's interests at the Peace Conference. He gave his support and proposed setting up a Special Commission of Plenipotentiaries, to be advised by a commission of women, appointed by the Inter-Allied Suffrage Conference, to inquire into, and report on, questions which were of international importance to women. It is interesting to note that the International Woman Suffrage Alliance was amongst those instrumental in securing representation of women at the Peace Conference in 1919 and subsequently at the League of Nations.

Millicent Fawcett, Mrs Oliver Smith and Rosamund Smith represented Britain at the original conference. Millicent Fawcett was unable to attend the Peace Conference and she asked Margery Corbett Ashby to take her place. Margery Corbett Ashby was later to become president of the International Alliance of Women (1926/1946), and did much to form its policy. She remained a keen member of the IAW board during her long life and was actively involved in it and other women's organisations, working to enhance the status of women until her death at the age of 96. She was made a Dame of the British Empire in 1967 in recognition of her work to improve conditions for women, not only in Britain but all over the world. Dame Margery was a good friend to the IHA over the years. She entered Newnham College Cambridge in 1901, and received her degree from Trinity College Dublin in 1904. Oxford and Cambridge did not confer degrees on women at that time, Trinity College was the link with Ireland which she was proud to acknowledge.

IAW held its first post-war congress in Interlaken in 1946. In her presidential address at Interlaken Margery Corbett Ashby assessed the progress made since the last congress held in Copenhagen in 1939. Women had acquired political equality in most countries and had lost their sense of inferiority; the United

Nations had proclaimed sex equality as a human right necessary for the attainment of peace, liberty and economic security. On the debit side: women were still paid less than men for equal work or work requiring equal skill; posts of responsibility in government, the professions and industry were not given to women. Margery stated that the legal and economic position of married women was 'profoundly unsatisfactory' and that this was 'our largest unsolved problem'.(See Whittick, 1979.)

During the period of the Second World War, 1939-1945, IAW was unable to hold its yearly board meetings and triennial congresses, but kept contact with affiliates and distributed its paper, *The International Women's News*, as best it could under war conditions. Due to these contacts IAW was able to resume work as soon as peace was restored.

In 1949 the IHA was represented for the first time at the IAW Congress held in Amsterdam by Andrée Sheehy Skeffington, Beryl Carr Lett, Ruth Deale and myself. This was the first time since 1939 that we had been out of Ireland and we were horrified at the devastation still to be seen in Holland where the great port of Rotterdam was being rebuilt. We were taken to see the various social services set up to deal with the effects of the war on the people.

At the Amsterdam Congress IAW expressed 'profound satisfaction' that in the Charter of the United Nations and the Universal Declaration of Human Rights 'the nations of the world have recognised the principle for which the Alliance stands, namely equality between men and women' and called upon the UN 'to take urgent steps to secure the implementation of the principle'.

The work of the Alliance is carried out by five commissions which prepare the resolutions to be passed at congress, as follows: Peace and the United Nations, Civil and Political Rights, Economic Rights, Equal Moral Standards, Equal Education Rights. Between the triennial congresses the board of IAW, consisting of the president, officers and members, elected at each congress by the delegates from affiliated organisations, meet each year in different countries where there are affiliates. Each affiliate appoints a person, or committee, to correspond with the convenor of the various IAW commissions, to reply to questionnaires and to give reports on conditions in their countries relevant to the commissions.

We returned from the congress greatly cheered to find that women in other countries were facing the same problems. Only the emphasis differed, depending on the conditions for women in each country. With renewed enthusiasm the international committee of the IHA set up networks to liaise with the commissions of IAW and to monitor laws and conditions affecting women in Ireland.

Our first effort was to press for equal pay. We made representations to the government and the trade unions, but the only support came from Louie Bennett and the Women Workers Union. We were particularly disappointed by the attitude of the trade unions. They just did not want to hear about equal pay. However, we need not have been so shocked by this as we discovered that many married women felt that equal pay for women was a direct threat to their husbands' jobs. It was the same with other reforms we hoped to initiate. Women were nervous about innovations; we had to gain their support first.

After the Amsterdam Congress in 1949 the Irish Housewives were represented at IAW congresses at Naples (1952), Athens (1955), Dublin (1961), Trieste (1964), London (1967), Konigstein (1970), New Delhi (1973), New York (1976), Monrovia (1979), Helsinki (1982), Mauritius (1986), Melbourne (1989).

At the present time, (1992), the International Alliance of Women has Consultative Status B with the United Nations and has permanent representatives to the UN, including the ILO and WHO, at New York, Vienna and Geneva, to Unesco in Paris, and to FAO in Rome. There are affiliated organisations in fifty-two countries and associated societies in ten countries. To qualify for affiliation, an organisation has to be non-governmental. This stipulation has ruled out organisations subject to government control, though IAW has invited representatives from the Soviet Union and China to attend congresses as observers. To qualify for affiliation, organisations must be committed to advancing the status of women in their own country and worldwide. There are also individual members of IAW who do not belong to any other organisation or live in countries where there are no affiliates. Individual members are invited to attend congresses but have no vote. They receive the *International Women's News*, published quarterly by IAW.

In 1958 the IHA decided that our delegate to the congress in Athens, Una Byrne, then Chair of the international committee of IHA, should invite IAW to hold the next congress in Dublin in 1961. The invitation was accepted and with some trepidation we started to prepare for the congress.

In 1959 the president of IAW, Ezlynn Deraniyagala from Sri Lanka, and the secretary, Elizabeth Halsey from USA, came to Ireland to make arrangements and left us a blue-print for the planning of the congress.

We set to work at once. His Excellency, Eamonn de Valera, the President of Ireland, agreed to be patron of the congress. It was said to be the first time he had ever granted this honour to a women's organisation. Dr McQuaid, Archbishop of Dublin, lent us the Institute of Catholic Sociology as the venue for the congress, with the Dominican Hall, Eccles Street, for plenary sessions, the only conditions being that we should leave the premises as we had found them.

Dr Patrick Hillery, then Minister for Education, spoke at the opening ceremony and hosted a state reception at Iveagh House for the delegates. Mr de Valera invited the board of IAW and the organising committee of the IHA to tea at Aras an Uachtaráin. We were greatly impressed by Mrs de Valera's knowledge of the proceedings of the congress. She had followed closely the press reports of the various sessions.

The IHA gave a reception at the Mansion House at which Gráinne Yeats played the harp to entertain our guests. Mrs Summer-Hayes, wife of the USA ambassador to Sri Lanka and a friend of Ezlynn Deraniyagala, gave a party for the delegates and members of the IHA at Carton, which she and her husband had rented for the summer of 1961.

The IHA also arranged a day expedition to Killarney, including a trip round the lakes by jaunting car. This trip was marred by the death of Miss Anna Munro, a well-known British suffragette. Great credit was due to Lillie O'Callaghan, who organised the Killarney trip. She managed to keep the death from the other participants, so that their pleasure in the outing should not be spoiled. Miss Munro, who was in her nineties, had collapsed while climbing up on to a jaunting car, and died almost immediately. A happier expedition was arranged to Glendalough by Bord Fáilte who entertained the delegates to lunch there.

During the congress Miss Marian Reeves, then president of the Women's Freedom League, Mrs Corbett Ashby, Miss Anna Munro, Miss Lilian Thomas and other former suffragettes in Dublin for the Congress visited the Republican Plot in Glasnevin Cemetery to pay tribute to Charlotte Despard and lay flowers on her grave.

Charlotte Despard had been a member of the Women's Social and Political Union (WSPU) founded by Emmeline Pankhurst in 1903, but later became president of the Women's Freedom League (WFL). She came to Ireland from time to time to address public meetings and in 1917 met Maud Gonne McBride. In 1918 Charlotte Despard stood as the Labour candidate for Battersea but was not elected. Her brother, Sir John French, became Viceroy of Ireland and held the post until 1921, surviving an assassination attempt in 1919. In 1921 Mrs Despard left Battersea and settled permanently in Ireland. In 1922 the Civil War started, the Women Prisoners Defence League (WPDL), was set up and Mrs Despard moved into Roebuck House on the outskirts of Dublin, where Maud Gonne joined her the following year. The WPDL was proscribed and Maud Gonne imprisoned in Kilmainham Jail, Charlotte Despard organising a vigil outside. In the following years Charlotte Despard supported a variety of causes such as the republican protest against O'Casey's play, *The Plough and the Stars*. She was involved with the Irish Workers' Party, she was branded as a communist and at one time a dangerous subversive, and Roebuck House was raided.

In 1932 Charlotte campaigned for Eamonn de Valera who won the general election. In 1934 she moved to the North and took part in anti-fascist demonstrations and in 1936 supported the republican side in the Spanish Civil War. In 1939, shortly after the outbreak of the Second World War, Charlotte Despard died after a fall in her home. She was aged ninety-five. Her friends decided they would fulfil her wish to be buried in Glasnevin Cemetery in Dublin. The funeral cortege set out from Whitehead in Antrim and had reached huge proportions by the time it reached Dublin, all shades of left-wing republican politics being represented. Women turned out in force. Maud Gonne made the funeral oration. Hanna Sheehy Skeffington represented the Women's Freedom league and laid their wreath on her grave. It was fitting that Charlotte should be remembered by the women attending the IAW congress, several of whom had campaigned with her for the vote in England. Irish women today might more often remember the part she played in the advancement of the rights of women.

These details of the organisation of the congress show the great interest and co-operation of the government and state bodies in the event. The press gave very full coverage of the congress. We also remember the interest and friendliness of the ordinary people of Dublin who welcomed and helped our guests in a very real way, and the many who came to Eccles Street each day to see the women from abroad in their colourful costumes.

The hard work and dedication of the various organising committees of the IHA paid off because the congress ran very smoothly, and IAW still refers to the Dublin Congress as a model congress! All our members worked with enthusiasm but special mention must go to Eileen Hackett, vice-chairwoman, whose job was to co-ordinate the work of the committees. Eileen was continuously on duty throughout the congress and managed to solve all problems with a smile. Edith Cellem, joint honorary secretary, acted as PRO and set up a relationship with the press which resulted in excellent coverage of all congress sessions and social events. Mary Meagher who for so many years had run our social committee which organised our main fund-raising events, and her faithful band of helpers, ran the cafeteria in the basement of the Institute of Catholic Sociology and provided lunch and tea every day for 350 delegates, as well as the extra 'cuppa' day or night!

At the time of the congress the IHA had about 500 members and the experience of working together united them and helped them realise what women could do by co-operation. As a result of the publicity many women who had attended open sessions of the congress joined the IHA. We also benefitted materially because one of our members, Jim Petrie, had organised an exhibition for manufacturers of Irish goods at our reception in the Mansion House, to help defray some of our expenses. The result was that we had 400 pounds to add to our funds when the final reckoning with IAW was completed.

However, the greatest asset was the increased respect the IHA had gained in the eyes of the government and the public generally. It is the policy of IAW, when holding a congress or board meeting in a country, to highlight specific problems of that particular country, and Ireland was no exception.

In 1961 women in Britain as well as in Ireland had been disturbed by the case of a man in England who having had 'carnal knowledge' of a twelve-year-old girl, brought her to Ireland and married her to avoid prosecution in England. (The marriage age in Ireland at that time was twelve.)

The IHA, together with the Joint committee of Women's Societies and Social Workers, had asked the government to raise the marriage age to correspond with canon law (fourteen for girls and sixteen for boys), but without success. The IHA took the opportunity to discuss the matter at the congress and advocated that a minimum age of eighteen for both sexes would be preferable. The question of the marriage age was hotly debated in many letters to newspapers, some saying that it was necessary that a pregnant girl of twelve should be married to give legitimacy to the child, while IAW took the view that early marriage militated against free consent. It was suggested that ideally a minimum age should be decided internationally, but that it was necessary to comply with the various customs in each country. The debate helped to awaken public awareness to this problem and eventually the marriage age was raised to sixteen (for both sexes) in the Marriage Act of 1972.

Two other issues for which the IHA and other organisations had been campaigning were the need for women police, and jury service for women on the same terms as men. Both subjects were raised at the congress, but no government action was taken. The usual excuses were made: no toilet facilities for women in the Garda barracks; women could not leave their young children to serve on juries. Two of our members, Beatrice Dixon and Kathleen Swanton, who qualified as householders, had succeeded in being called for jury service in 1959, but both had been objected to on several occasions until Beatrice Dixon finally succeeded. Women had been pressing for women police since the twenties and our first chairwoman, Susan Manning, told me that she with her sister, Louie Bennett, and other women of the time had patrolled the streets in the evening during the time of the Civil War, to safeguard women.

Other issues discussed at the Dublin Congress were means to achieve a better proportion of women in national parliaments and the inclusion of Article 16 of the Universal Declaration of Human Rights in Article 22 of the Draft Convention on Civil and Political Rights. Article 16 states that men and women 'are entitled to equal rights as to marriage, during marriage and at its dissolution'. This was sent as a resolution to the UN and delegates were asked to request the leaders of their national delegations to the next UN General Assembly to support this. Another item was the age of retirement and pension rights. Affiliated societies were requested to 'take steps to educate and convince women workers of their ultimate advantage in acquiring an equal age of retirement and equal pension rights with men'. It is interesting to note how long it has taken to realise so many of these aspirations.

At the Dublin Congress I was elected to the board of IAW. At the time I was chairwoman of the IHA. The IHA welcomed the appointment 'as long as it did not cost the IHA anything'. I served for three years but did not stand for election in 1964 due to financial constraints. I was again elected to the IAW board in 1973 in India and served until 1989. During that period I was appointed convenor of the IAW Commission on International Understanding (Peace through Human Rights and International Understanding), and in that capacity represented IAW as an observer at the UN General Assembly Second Session on Disarmament (New York, 1982); UN Peace Expert Meeting (Vienna, 1984); UN Regional Meeting to prepare for UN

International Year of Peace (Vienna, 1985); UN NGO Conference to open UN International Year of Peace (Geneva, 1986) and I accompanied the president of IAW and two vice-presidents to China at the invitation of the All China Women's Federation.

In 1977 IAW held a board meeting in Dublin at Trinity Hall. This was hosted by the IHA who gave a reception to enable members of other women's organisations to meet the board members.

In 1978 the Council for the Status of Women (CSW), applied for membership of IAW and the IHA was delighted to have more Irish representation on IAW. The Women's Political Association had been affiliated to IAW for a period during the '70s and was represented at the congress in New York in 1976. In 1989 Caroline McCamley of CSW was elected to the board of IAW and I was made an honorary member.

One of the difficulties for Irish board members has been the high cost of travelling to board meetings in different parts of the world, as government grants have not been available. This also applies to congress delegates who have always had to pay their own expenses. Most other countries which have affiliated societies acknowledge the importance of representation at IAW meetings by giving government grants to the delegates, at least to the extent of providing the air fare. This lack of funding effectively prevents Irish board members standing for the executive of IAW.

In 1986 as Convenor of the IAW Commission on International Understanding, I organised a Workshop on Peace through Human Rights and International Understanding for the European Region of IAW at the Bellinter Conference Centre in Navan to mark the UN International Year of Peace. Its success was largely due to the help and co-operation of CSW and IHA. Delegates from seven European countries attended as well as women from both communities in Northern Ireland and from the Republic. The need to resolve conflict without resorting to violence was stressed as well as the necessity for education to lead a life in peace.

Drive for a national commission

In 1967 a delegation from the IHA attended the IAW congress, held that year in London. There the delegates were told that the UN Commission on the Status of Women had issued a directive to women's international non-governmental organisations to ask their affiliates to examine the status of women in their own countries and, where necessary, urge their governments to set up a national commission on the status of women.

When the IHA delegation returned to Ireland Nora Browne, who is a member of IHA, told us that the Business and Professional Women's Clubs had received the same directive at their international congress held in Copenhagen the same year, which she had also attended as a delegate. After discussion with the Business and Professional Women's Club (established to set up and maintain standards for women in business and the professions while safeguarding their interests in areas such as equal pay and equal opportunities), we decided to work together on the project of setting up a National Commission on the Status of Women in Ireland.

Accordingly a meeting was organised by the international sub-committee of the Irish Housewives Association in conjuction with the BPW and held in the Central Hotel, Dublin, on 30 January 1968. Maude Rooney, chairwoman of the IHA, presided and the following women's organisations were represented: The Business and Professional Women's Association (BPW), Altrusa Club (an international services club), Irish Countrywomen's Association (ICA), Irish Nursing Organisation (INO), Irish Housewives Association (IHA), Dublin University Women Graduates Association (DUWGA), The Irish Widows Association, The Soroptimists' Clubs of Ireland, Women's International Zionist Organisation (WIZO), Irish Council of Women, Association of Women Citizens,

Association of Secondary Teachers of Ireland (ASTI). The Women Graduates of University College Dublin were unable to attend but asked to be informed of the outcome of the meeting. The Joint Committee of Women's Societies and Social Workers did not attend because being a representative body, many of their members would be there from their own organisations. Miss Rosaleen Mills was invited in her own right as an established feminist, the veteran of many campaigns in women's causes; as a young girl she had been involved with the suffragette movement.

The points for consideration at the meeting were the drawing up of a Women's Charter and the need for a National Commission on the Status of Women. Each delegate was asked in turn to speak on these two topics. After much discussion it was agreed to drop the idea of a Women's Charter and concentrate on researching the need for a national commission. Mrs Beatrice Grosvenor, president of the Irish Federation of Soroptimists Clubs, proposed, and Mrs Jon Clayton, vice-president of the BPW, seconded, that an *ad hoc* committee be set up to work for a limited period, to research the need for a national commission. This proposal was adopted unanimously and it was agreed that each organisation present should be invited to nominate one member to the *ad hoc* committee.

The first meeting of the *ad hoc* committee was held on 12 March, 1968, at the rooms of the Dublin University Women Graduates Association (DUWGA), which had offered its premises as a venue for the *ad hoc* Committee. Eileen Hackett, chairwoman of the international committee of the IHA, welcomed members and asked for nominations for officers. The following were elected: chairwoman: Hilda Tweedy (IHA), honorary secretary: Dr Blanche Weekes (BPW), honorary treasurer: Dr Hazel Boland (WIZO). Permanent members of the *ad hoc* committee were: Association of Irish Widows: Eileen Proctor, Association of Women Citizens: Evelyn Owens, BPW Clubs: Nora Browne, Irish Council of Women: Ena Cahill, Irish Countrywomen's Association: Kathleen Delap, Irish Housewives Association: Eileen Hackett, Soroptimists: Beatrice Grosvenor, Women Graduates, TCD: Blanche Weekes, Women Graduates, UCD: Geraldine Roche, WIZO: Hazel Boland, Independent:

Rosaleen Mills. Each organisation could appoint a proxy who could attend meetings, but only one vote per organisation was allowed. Each organisation paid one pound to cover stationery, postage and the final report. DUWGA provided their room free of charge.

Having discussed the possibility of holding a seminar and addressing women's organisations on the need for setting up a National Commission on the Status of Women, it was finally decided not to seek publicity for the work we hoped to do, but to confine our research to the data supplied by the constituent organisations of the *ad hoc* Committee, in order to comply with the time limit stipulated at the original meeting.

It was decided that delegates should monitor advertisements and note those which offered less pay to women when the qualifications for, and specifications of, the job were the same. It was agreed that women had to be educated to expect equal pay. Many were traditional in their outlook and accepted that they would not be paid the same as men. Many married women looked on equal pay as a threat to their husbands' livelihood. The dilemma was that women might get the jobs if they were a source of cheap labour, while with equal pay, men would get preference.

Discrimination against married women in the areas of obtaining employment, paying income tax and exploitation in part-time work as well as pensions and retirement age, were also subjects for investigation. The availability of educational facilities for girls wishing to do courses in science and higher mathematics in preparation for non-traditional jobs, and of training and re-training in employment, were hotly debated subjects. The question of the composition and terms of reference of the proposed national commission had been discussed by the various organisations and consensus was beginning to emerge.

At a specially called meeting of the *ad hoc* committee on 28 May 1968 we heard through the Association of Women Citizens' Newsletter that : 'At its Annual General Meeting in Killarney the ICTU will debate whether the government should be asked to set up a Commission to enquire into the Status of Women. The officers of the Association have been working in close touch with other women's organisations, Trinity Women Graduates, Dublin Business and Professional Women's Clubs, etc'. Evelyn Owens, who with her proxy, Helen Burke, were officers of the ICTU, had mentioned that this resolution would be debated at the ICTU meeting, but unfortunately were not able to attend our meeting at short notice.

The implications of this action by the ICTU was discussed and it was decided to make a press statement as we did not want to follow the ICTU, though we much appreciated their support. It was important that the demand for a National Commission on the Status of Women should come from women's organisations, as Evelyn Owens had stated previously. Accordingly the following statement was sent to the press :

'Since January of this year an *ad hoc* committee formed by members of the women's organisations listed hereunder has been considering the status of women in Ireland and discussing the advisability of approaching the government to set up a national commission on the Status of Women.

'This Committee has been studying the legal, political, civil and economic position of women and gathering relevant information. Anyone who is in a position to supply factual information likely to be of use to this Committee is invited to communicate with the Chairman, Mrs Hilda Tweedy, or with the Hon Secretary, Dr Blanche Weekes.' A list of the member organisations was included.

At the next meeting on 6 June 1968, it was reported that the statement had appeared in three national papers and that there were enquiries from women's magazines, journalists, and individual women. Evelyn Owens wrote to say that the resolution had been unanimously passed by the ICTU conference and that the executive would pass the resolution to Dr Hillery, then Minister for Labour.

It was decided that it was now time for the *ad hoc* committee to write a memorandum for presentation to the Taoiseach, Mr Jack Lynch, and to request him to set up a National Commission on the Status of Women. These decisions greatly concentrated our minds and a schedule was set for a meeting on 9 July to approve the memorandum, which would then be sent to our organisations for approval, and a following meeting on 8 October 1968 would finalise the memoradum and arrange for its presentation to the Taoiseach.

During research the *ad hoc* committee had studied the UN Declaration on the Elimination of Discrimination against Women and had related the various points to the situation of women in Ireland. Concern was expressed that Ireland had not signed and ratified the UN conventions of particular interest to women. The position regarding the conventions in October 1968 was as follows: Equal Pay: signed and ratified, but not implemented. Abolition of Slavery: agreed to, but not signed. Traffic in persons: agreed to, but not signed. Marriage (consent, minimum age, and registration): agreed to, but not signed. Recognition and enforcement abroad of maintenance obligations: Ireland has a reciprocal agreement with Britain, so no more was necessary, according to the government. In view of this position it was decided to ask for the signing, ratification and implementation of these UN conventions in the memorandum.

The memorandum was sent to the Taoiseach, Mr Lynch, after our meeting on 8 October 1968, and a letter asking him to receive a deputation to discuss it.

Then came the long wait. First there was the usual acknowledgement from the Taoiseach's department. On 12 December 1968 we received a letter from Mr Lynch stating he had received the documents but it would not be possible for him to meet us until after the New Year. On 11 March 1969 we wrote again to the Taoiseach. As no reply was received after ten days the following letter was sent to the leaders of the opposition:

'The enclosed memorandum has been prepared by a committee representing the undermentioned women's organisations and has already been sent to the Taoiseach. We would welcome your views on the setting up of a National Commission on the Status of Women.'

At our meeting on 10 April 1969 it was reported that Mr Lynch had replied, saying the matter would receive his attention when he had time. Mr Cosgrave, Fine Gael, stated that he had put down a parliamentary question to the Taoiseach and would send us his reply. Mr Corish, Labour, arranged that some of our members should meet Mrs Eileen Desmond TD, to discuss the points of the memorandum with her.

This waiting period was very frustrating for the *ad hoc* committee, but we worked steadily on. We lobbied the candidates for the 1969 Dáil elections, asking them to support the setting-up of a commission. We continued to monitor advertisements for employment in the context of equal pay and other forms of discrimination against women. It was during this period that the question of battered wives was first brought to our attention in a memorandum from a country branch of one of our organisations. Until then women had been reluctant to speak about the violence in their homes. We also gathered information about commissions on the status of women in Denmark and in Canada, which helped us determine the type of commission we desired. We decided that the commission should consist of an equal number of men and women, with an independent chairwoman, Dr Thekla Beere, being suggested.

At a meeting on 28 October 1969 the *ad hoc* committee decided to write again to Mr Lynch asking him to receive a deputation. We also arranged to hold a press conference to make a statement and publish the memorandum on 12 November 1968.

On Friday, 7 November 1969, we received a letter from Mr Lynch saying that he was recommending to the government the setting-up of a National Commission on the Status of Women and that he would announce this when he was speaking to a women's group in Cork the following day. So the National Commission on the Status of Women was announced at the annual dinner of the Soroptimists Clubs.

On 12 November we wrote to Mr Lynch expressing our pleasure at his announcement but stressing that the *ad hoc* committee still felt it was important that he should receive our deputation and we enclosed a copy of our press release.

On 9 December 1969 we wrote to Mr Lynch: 'The *Ad Hoc* Committee learns with surprise and distress that a suggestion has been made by the official side at a General Council Meeting of the Civil Service that certain pay-claims in the Public Service, which are based on the principle of equal pay for work of equal value - a principle to which the Government has declared itself sympathetic - should be referred to the Commission on the Status of Women, a Commission which has not as yet been set up, and whose mandate and terms of reference are unknown. The *Ad Hoc* Committee had frankly never envisaged this possibility. The Government, acknowledging a grievance, has within itself the power to rectify the grievance. The members of the *Ad Hoc* Committee deplore the suggestion that the setting up of a Commission should be used to delay action on any of the points mentioned in our Memorandum. We consider the setting up of the Commission a matter of great urgency and we trust that the Government will not delay action in this matter.

'We were disappointed that you have not been able to meet the *Ad Hoc* Committee. The Officers of the Committee will attend at Leinster House on the afternoon of Tuesday, 16 December, and, should you be unavailable, again on Wednesday, 17, when perhaps you can see your way to consult with them regarding matters raised in this letter. We would point out that the *Ad Hoc* Committee is not an individual group but one whose members, as representatives of their organisations, cover the whole range of women's interests in Ireland. We would reiterate that we feel that it would be of immense importance to discuss the composition and terms of reference of the Commission with you before its setting up, and we feel strongly that the Commission should be equally representative of men and women. We consider it essential that the women's organisations, through the *Ad Hoc* Committee, should be represented on the Commission.'

It was decided to send a copy of this letter to all the daily and Sunday papers on 11 December. We also arranged which members of the committee would attend the Dáil to meet Mr Lynch on 16 or 17 December 1969.

Before that letter was posted the *ad hoc* committee had been invited to meet Mr Haughey, the Minister for Finance, under whose auspices the commission was to be set up. The following represented the *ad hoc* committee : Dr Boland (WIZO), Mrs Browne (BPW), Mrs Delap (ICA), Dr Weekes (DUWGA), Mrs Tweedy (IHA). At the meeting Mr Haughey expressed the goodwill of the government and said the setting up of the commission was imminent. He agreed that the terms of reference should be as wide as possible and that the membership of the commission should be half men and half women and consist of about fifteen people. We said that the chair should be a woman, and Mr Haughey suggested the names of Fianna Fáil women who were in the Dáil or Senate, but we stressed that the chair must be independent of party affiliations and stated that we wanted the most suitable person for the job; we believed this to be Dr Thekla Beere.

Dr Thekla Beere had a remarkable career in the Ireland of that time. Born into a Church of Ireland rector's family, she had been seriously ill as a child, so she had no formal education until she was fourteen, when she went to Alexandra School and College. Her mother, who had herself wanted to study medicine, had encouraged Thekla to study at home during her illness and was determined that Thekla would have the educational opportunities that she herself had missed. Thekla Beere entered Trinity College Dublin in 1919 where she studied law and legal and political science and distinguished herself academically in an area very unusual for women of the time. Thekla was the only woman student in the law school. With these high qualifications she found it difficult to find a job, but eventually started as a third-grade clerk in Central Statistics, at a meagre salary. Meanwhile she had applied for a scholarship to study in America and was awarded a two-year Rockfeller Scholarship. Thekla made good use of her time and studied in Washington and Chicago, as well as Berkeley College in California and Harvard in Boston. Returned to Ireland she joined the civil service and worked her way upwards until she reached the highest position a woman has ever attained in Ireland. She became parliamentary secretary to a government department, the Department of Transport and Power, but throughout her career never attained equal pay with her male colleagues. Thekla maintained that the secret of her success was not great intellectual strength (which she had in abundance), but the fact that she was determined and always took an opportunity when it arose. Thekla never described herself as a feminist. In the early days she was too busy working. She had to give private grinds to survive when she was studying and to supplement her income in the lower ranks of the civil service. She did not find noticeable discrimination against her in her own career, although she always tried to see that women who were under her in the civil service were justly treated. When offered the position of chair of the Commission on the Status of Women, Thekla accepted as a matter of duty. She had reached the top. She wanted to help other women.

In our interview with Mr Haughey, he had asked us to submit four names from the *ad hoc* committee from which he would choose two. The names of Dr Boland, Mrs Browne, Mrs Delap and Mrs Tweedy were put forward as agreed by the *ad hoc* committee. Mrs Browne and Mrs Delap were duly appointed. Mr Haughey said that the commission would not be permanent, but would sit over a long period, reporting at intervals.

At a meeting on 9 February 1970 it was decided to write to Mr Haughey before he presented the budget. We wanted to make it quite clear to the government that the setting up of the commission should not be used as an excuse for delaying reforms in the financial area. In our letter we raised the following points:
(1) That the married woman, whether working inside, or outside the home, should have the same income tax allowance, ie, for married couples the income tax allowance should be double the single person's allowance.
(2) That the joint income of a married couple is the result of their joint efforts and it is unfair that it should be regarded as the property of one for the purposes of estate duty. No estate duty on the surviving spouse's share should be payable until both spouses are dead.
(3) That adequate allowances for widow and deserted or separated wife should be made, so that she may be in a position to keep her children with her.

On 4 April 1970 the terms of reference of the Commission were published:
'To examine and report on the status of women in Irish society, to make recommendations on the steps necessary to ensure the participation of women on equal terms with men in the political, social, cultural and economic life of the country, and to indicate

the implications generally - including the estimated cost - of such recommendations.'

The following appointments to the commission were also announced: chair - Dr Thekla Beere, former Secretary of the Department of Transport and Power; members - Mr Rory Barnes, managing director, Glen Abbey, Ltd; Mrs Nora Browne, *ad hoc* committee; Mrs Sheila Conroy, former member of the national executive of the General Workers' Union; Mrs Kathleen Delap, *ad hoc* committee; Mr William J Fitzpatrick, secretary, Irish Union of Distributive Workers and Clerks; Professor Michael Fogarty, director, Economic and Social Research Institute; Mrs Kathleen Gleeson, Farm Home Management adviser, County Cork Committee of Agriculture; Miss Eileen Kennedy, Justice of the district court; Mr Daniel J McAuley, economic officer, Federated Union of Employers; Mrs Alice McTernan, housewife and member of the Irish Countrywomen's Association; Mr Patrick Philip O'Donoghue, SC; Lt General Sir Geoffrey Thompson, former director, Arthur Guinness, Son and Company Ltd who was later replaced by Brian S Pim. The Minister appointed Mr Liam O Direáin, of the Department of Finance, to be secretary to the commission.

The *ad hoc* committee met on 5 May 1970 to wind up our affairs as we had attained the purpose for which we had been set up. Satisfaction was expressed that Mrs Browne and Mrs Delap would represent us on the commission. Satisfaction was also expressed with the composition of the commission generally, and with the terms of reference. A letter was sent to the commission with our wishes for its success and asking that the matters mentioned in our memorandum should be given priority in their deliberations.

Letters were sent to the constituent women's organisations saying that the *ad hoc* committee was now dissolved and asking each organisation to continue collecting information relevant to the terms of reference of the commission which could be given as evidence to it. It was decided that the former members of the *ad hoc* committee should be called together to consider the report of the commission when issued.

This account of the *ad hoc* committee, most of which has

been taken from the minutes book of the committee, (which is to be deposited in the Women's Archive), has been given here because the Irish Housewives Association was deeply involved in the work of the committee, as were all the other constituent organisations, doing research and back-up work. The delegates forming the committee all worked unsparingly and a great feeling of solidarity between the various organisations grew up. The work of the *ad hoc* committee became part of the history of each organisation.

The IHA prepared evidence which was presented orally to the commission. Our evidence dealt mostly with the problems of women in the home, particularly those regarding family law and the financial status of the married woman, whether she worked in the home or outside it, stressing the need for creches and nursery schools which are as necessary to the woman working in the home as to the woman working outside it.

In August 1971 the Commission on the Status of Women presented an Interim Report on Equal Pay to the Minister for Finance as had been requested by him on 19 June 1970. With Ireland's entry into the EEC and the UN interest in the status of women, it was becoming urgent that the government should make some reforms to bring Ireland in line with the directives of the EEC.

The full report of the commission was published in December 1972 and the former members of the *ad hoc* committee were called together to assess it. We at once realised that this was a blue-print for reform which would go a long way to satisfy women in Ireland, and that the constituent organisations had a responsibility to ensure that the recommendations of the report were implemented. It was decided that a letter should be sent to the press expressing satisfaction with the report and inviting interested organisations to join us to set up a permanent Council on the Status of Women to monitor the implementation of the recommendations of the report and deal with subsequent instances of discrimination.

The most controversial recommendation was the one on family planning. This issue was not included in the *ad hoc* memorandum because the debate on family planning was very divisive at that time. Not only would the representatives of the constituent organisations be unable to reach consensus on family planning, the organisations themselves had no stated policy.

The national commission received 'representations concerning family planning from several organisations and individuals, but principally from the Irish Family Planning Rights Association and the Fertility Guidance Co Ltd.' The Irish Family Planning Rights Association argued 'that husband and wife have the right to decide on the number and spacing of their family and the right to access to information and reliable means towards this end.' The Fertility Guidance Co Ltd was non-profit making and operated two clinics under medical supervision in Dublin, giving advice on all methods of family planning.

The national commission decided that the subject of family planning came within its terms of reference as it is included in the programme of work of the UN Commission on the Status of Women. At the UN International Conference on Human Rights held in Teheran in 1968 it was proclaimed that 'parents have a basic human right to determine freely and responsibly the number and spacing of their children' and a resolution of the conference considered that couples have a right to 'adequate education and information' in this respect. It is interesting to note that the Resolution was adopted with forty-nine votes for, none against and seven absentions. Ireland voted for the resolution.

The UN Declaration on Social Progress and Development in 1969 drew attention to 'the formulation and establishment, as needed, of programmes in the field of population, within the framework of national demographic policies and as part of the medical welfare services, including education, training of personnel and the provision to families of the knowledge and means necessary to enable them to exercise their right to determine freely and reasonably the number and spacing of their children.' Before the vote Ireland intervened to point out that the inclusion of the words 'and means' created 'difficulties of a moral character' for a number of delegations and asked for a vote on their inclusion. The words were retained with sixty for, sixteen against (including Ireland), and seventeen abstentions. The declaration was finally adopted as a whole with 119 votes for (including Ireland), none against and two abstentions.

After much debate the commission declared in paragraph 572 of the report, 'We consider that parents have the right to regulate the number and spacing of their family and that such right can only be exercised with the full agreement of both husband and wife and is not the exclusive right of one or the other.' It also declared 'We recommend, accordingly, that:

(1) Information and expert advice on family planning should be available through medical and other appropriate channels to families throughout the country. Such advice should respect the moral and personal attitudes of each married couple. (2) Medical requirements arising out of the married couples' decisions on family planning should be available under control and through channels to be determined by the Department of Health.' (See Commission on the Status of Women Report, December 1972, paragraphs 568 to 574.)

Many women's organisations, not least the IHA, had great difficulty in accepting this recommendation as there was no consensus amongst members. Our principle has always been not to press for consensus on moral issues, but we have also adhered to the principle that women have the right to information to make their individual decisions. This principle also held in the recent debate on abortion when the IHA stated that, while in no way advocating abortion, information should be available.

The IHA organised a luncheon to celebrate the publication of the report of the commission at which Dr Thekla Beere was the guest of honour. The Minister for Finance also attended and spoke on the implementation of the Beere Report. At the luncheon an elderly lady remarked 'If I had realised how I had been discriminated against, things would have been different'

Council for the Status of Women

The *ad hoc* committee on the Status of Women, having met again to consider the Interim Report of the National Commission on the Status of Women, decided that it would be necessary to form a permanent Council on the Status of Women to ensure the implementation of the recommendations of the report of the commission. Accordingly we wrote to the press in October 1972 inviting interested women's organisations to join with the nucleus of the *ad hoc* committee to form the Council for the Status of Women (CSW).

The objective of the council was the implementation of the report, *de jure* and *de facto*, and to deal with specific cases of discrimination against women as these arose. It also saw the need to educate the public to accept women as equal citizens and to break down prejudice in customs and practice.

Our priority would be to work for a change in the law, where necessary. Change in the law is the first most important step, but after that is monitoring the implementation of the law and creating an acceptance of the changes made. This is a huge and on-going task, making women aware of their human and civil rights so that they are prepared to claim them.

During this period, the late sixties and early seventies, while the *ad hoc* committee was functioning and at the time the Council for the Status of Women was founded, a parallel women's movement had evolved, almost unknown to the *ad hoc* group, out of which grew the Irish Women's Liberation Movement, and later, Irish Women United, which organised the famous 'contraceptive train' to Belfast in May 1972. (Contraceptives were banned in the Republic of Ireland, so forty-seven women travelled to Northern Ireland to buy contraceptives of all kinds and 'import' them to the South. This venture gave great publicity to the demand for a change in the law on contraception.)

Young women, most of them journalists, met in a large room over Gaj's Restaurant in Baggot Street, Dublin, and discussed the injustices suffered by Irish women. They decided to take action, drawing attention to discriminations against women. The group included Mary Maher, June Levine, Máirín de Burca, Nuala Fennell, Mary Anderson, Mary Kenny, Dr Máire Woods, Róisín Conroy, Nell McCafferty, Eavan Boland, Dr Eimer Philbin Bowman, Mairin Johnston, Bernadette Quinn and many others, including Hilary Boyle, journalist and broadcaster, a much older woman, who joined, or marched, in many causes related to justice for the under-privileged, amongst whom she counted women. Most of these women have made their mark in Ireland today and will not be forgotten.

There was considerable tension between the two women's movements, although both were basically working for the same objectives. The new group of justifiably angry young women, who expected immediate responses to their demands, looked upon the *ad hoc* committee, and the CSW, as 'establishment', and anything we did, or had done, was suspect to them. The CSW group resented the value of their work being negated and feared that the methods used by the younger group would result in a backlash which would further delay the reforms we all desired.

Members of the CSW studied the pamphlet *Chains or Change* produced by the Women's Liberation Movement, and later, *Banshee*, the magazine of Irish Women United, and found that these groups were pinpointing areas of discrimination which needed investigation and which the Council should address. However, there were confrontations on occasions. Nell McCafferty descended on the CSW committee on more than one occasion and told us in no uncertaim terms what we should be doing, but she did this in her own humourous style which left no rancour behind.

By 1975 when CSW held a seminar to mark International Women's Year, we were anxious to give a platform to the new groups, and shortly afterwards many of them joined the Council. AIM, founded by Nuala Fennell, to deal with family law and marital break-down, and the Women's Liberation Movement were founder members of CSW, and Cherish, a support group for single mothers, joined shortly afterwards.

At the UN Conference in Mexico Irish women were considered very advanced because we had an umbrella organisation like CSW which covered such a wide spectrum of women's organisations, even though we lagged sadly behind in matters of law. So, gradually the two groups in Ireland came to recognise that both were facets of the same movement and to respect each other. In 1992 the CSW has ninety affiliates, representing every aspect of women's aspirations.

It was stimulating and exciting for those who had been working since the thirties and forties to see the goals we had been struggling to attain become part of our legal system, largely through the work of Senator Mary Robinson, SC (now Her Excellency, the President of Ireland). The upsurge of interest amongst younger women gave a great fillip to the women's movement. There was a proliferation of new organisations, some to deal with just one specific issue. A number of these groups did not survive but they all played their part and are now part of women's history.

In October 1972 the Council for the Status of Women was formed by the following organisations: AIM, Altrusa, Association of Women Citizens of Ireland, Business and Professional Women's Clubs, Chartered Society of Physiotherapists, Cork Federation of Women's Organisations, Dublin University Women Graduates Association, Irish Countrywomen's Association, Irish Association of Dieticians, Irish Housewives Association, Irish Widows Association, National University Women Graduates Association, Soroptimists Clubs of Ireland, Women's International Zionist Organisation, Women's Liberation Movement, Women's Progressive Association (later Women's Political Association), ZONTA.

The Council re-elected the executive officers of the *ad hoc* committee as follows, with the exception of Dr Blanche Weekes, who did not wish to stand owing to pressure of other work - chairwoman: Hilda Tweedy; honorary treasurer: Dr Hazel Boland; honorary secretary: Margaret Waugh (founder member of the WPA). Here tribute must be paid to Dr Blanche Weekes who never spared herself as honorary secretary of the *ad hoc* committee. We were sorry that she did not stand for election to the Committee of the Council for the Status of Women, but pleased to see her there as a delegate representing BPW.

The Dublin University Women Graduates Association continued to provide their room in Trinity College free of charge. Only for their generosity, and later, that of the Irish Countrywomen's Association, who provided free accomodation at Merrion Road for our enlarged meetings, the Council could not have survived. We had no government grant and had to exist on the affiliation fees of our organisations. A quote from a letter from Monica Barnes, then honorary secretary, dated 10 July 1974, aptly described our financial plight after two years work, when we were desperately trying to launch a suitable programme for International Women's Year : 'It is such a shame we have not got the funds to get ourselves more publicity, we are running out of stamp money at the moment. But it (news of the UN International Women's Year) is filtering through to the public, and if we get government money, we can really launch ourselves.'

As soon as the Council was set up we immmediately wrote to the Minister for Finance, Mr Peter Barry, asking him to receive a deputation to discuss the question of equal pay in relation to the recommendations of the Interim Report of the National Commission on the Status of Women and the national wage agreement. We wrote to him again in March 1973 on the elimination of discrimination against women which we hoped would be reflected in the budget, asking that the following points be included : the implementation of equal pay for work of equal value as recommended in the Interim Report of the National Commission; the elimination of discrimination in income tax allowances and social welfare benefits for married women; provision for a full single person's tax allowance for married women whether working in the home or employed outside; the same tax allowance for the single parent with dependent children as for the married man.

On 8 May 1973 we wrote to the Taoiseach on a subject that has become far too familiar over the years: 'Mindful of your government's stated policy on elimination of discrimination against women and the poor representation of women in the new Oireachtas we trust that you will appoint a fair proportion of women on your panel for the Seanad'.

This was followed by a letter after the appointments were made in which we stated: 'We welcomed your assurance in the Senate debate that the government "was moving as rapidly as possible in every area in which Government action is needed", and agree whole-heartedly that "there are areas in which the prejudices or inherited traditions prevented the employment of women". We would point out, however, that this is one reason why we were so disappointed that you did not appoint at least one woman to your panel in the Senate. We believe that it is not enough for the Government to pass legislation, but that it should lead in removing prejudices by example'. How much has that situation changed in twenty years ?

On 30 May 1973 we sent the following letter to the Minister for Finance : 'We welcome the publication of the Report of the National Commission on the Status of Women, which we are studying in depth.

'We are particularly interested in the paragraphs on the setting up of a single body representing women's organisations interested in the Recommendations of the Report and to act as a liaison between Government Departments and the various organisations.

'We claim that the Council for the Status of Women (formed last September from the nucleus of the *ad hoc* committee on the Status of Women, which was instrumental in the setting up of the National Commission on the Status of Women), is such a body.

'We represent eighteen organisations (list attached), and we are hoping all organisations representative of men and women interested in raising the status of women in Ireland, will join us. Our terms of reference are to press for the implementation of the recommendations of the report and to deal with specific discriminations against women. We exchange information and co-ordinate the work of the various organisations dealing with different aspects of discrimination.

'At present we are studying the report with a view to

formulating a programme of work. One of the greatest needs is to publicise the recommendations and to educate the public, both men and women, to accept them in spirit as well as practice, and we look to the government to support us in this work. We shall submit a memorandum to you when we have studied the matter further. Meanwhile we seek recognition as the representative body that would carry out the work recommended in the report'.

We received an acknowledgement from the Minister saying that some of the recommendations were being implemented already, and that the remainder were under consideration by the departments concerned.

On 31 August 1973 we again wrote to Mr Richie Ryan, Minister for Finance, reminding him of our letter (copy above), in which we stated: 'Furthermore we wish to stress the importance of the Council being given recognition now, because it could be helpful to the different government departments which are now studying the report, in view of the amount of information which we have at our disposal through research by our member organisations.'

On 31 October 1973 we wrote to the Minister for Labour, Mr Michael O'Leary, stressing the importance of combining the legislation on equal pay with anti-discrimination clauses, 'otherwise benefit from equal pay may be negated. This could also avoid further legislation.'

We also sent the Minister a Memorandum on Proposed Legislation on Equal Pay for Women in which we suggested incorporation of anti-discrimination clauses such as prohibition of discrimination on the grounds of sex or marital status in respect of employment, trades and professions, education and training, so that there may be equal opportunity for all. We called for the phasing in of equal pay in graduated stages to be made obligatory and for equal basic rates for unskilled, semi-skilled and skilled categories and for female workers.

In relation to employment it should be illegal to discriminate by refusing to employ a person for work which is available and for which the person is qualified, with the exception of employment in private households; advertisements should be for persons, not male/female; employment and re-employment of married women should be facilitated; pregancy should be termed 'temporarily unfit' for work. We advocated equal treatment for men and women as regards terms of retirement and dependants. We touched on discrimination in trades and professions by refusal of membership or withholding membership rights, by withholding qualifications or failing to provide education or training.

We urged the setting up of a tribunal or board for disputes and claims for equal pay and opportunity. We suggested that government grants be withheld from employers failing to implement the Bill and that agricultural and domestic workers should come within the scope of the Bill.

For the remainder of 1973 and 1974 we continued to investigate and pass on to the government and other relevant bodies cases of discrimination against women. Likewise we continued to publicise the content of the recommendations of the report and press for their implementation.

At the beginning of December 1974 Mr Michael O'Leary, Minister for Labour, announced that he intended to set up the Women's Representative Committee to be the officially recognised body to represent women's interests, its functions to be: to monitor progress towards the implementation of the Recommendations of the Report of the Commission on the Status of Women; to make submissions on legislative and administrative reforms required to ensure that women participate in all spheres of life on equal terms with men; to maintain liaison with women's organisations and other bodies concerned with the elimination of discrimination against women; to act as a liaison body between government departments and individual women's organisations; to investigate and report on specific areas of discrimination against women which are brought to the attention of the committee by organisations or individual women; to identify areas of research on matters relevant to the status of women.

The Minister appointed Mrs Eileen Desmond, TD, to chair the Committee, the members to consist of four nominees of the Irish Congress of Trade Unions and the Federated Union of Employers, three nominees of the Council for the Status of

54

Women, one nominee of the Economic and Social Research Institute and a legal advisor nominated by the Minister. The Minister wrote to the Council of his intention and asked for the names of nominees. The Council welcomed the formation of the Women's Representative Committee and agreed to nominate three representatives. The CSW believed that this was the first step in gaining recognition as an umbrella organisation representing women's organisations. However, this did not please all the women's organisations and Gemma Hussey wrote to say the Women's Political Association had 'voted overwhelmingly to reject the Minister's proposals' and that ' AIM and Senator Robinson have publicly added their voices to protest against the Minister's actions'.

The Women's Political Association suggested that the Committee should consist of an expert from each area covered by the report which would 'enable the Committee to maintain a balanced programme and outlook'. Each expert should form a sub-committee of people with experience to carry out detailed studies in the area of concern and make specific proposals to the Committee, the following structure being suggested : 'Two from ICTU, one of which is a member of the Women's Advisory group; two from FUE, to concentrate on aspects of women in employment other than equal pay such as discrimination, training, provision of creches, maternity leave etc; one social worker or person used to dealing with specific problems of women, eg deserted wives, unmarried mothers; one specialist in family law. One woman with knowledge of, or experience in, public life, eg a woman who holds office in a political party, a lecturer in political science; one educationalist; one representative from the area of 'women in the home'; one representative of rural women, nominated by suitable organisations; one nominee from the Council for the Status of Women (to represent women's organisations); one civil servant appointment from the Department of Labour to co-ordinate between government departments; one ESRI nominee to assist with research and studies; a chair, a very eminent and determined *woman* whose appointment would give prestige to the Committee and ensure that it accomplished its objectives.'

The Council, having examined the suggestions put forward by the Women's Political Association, decided to hold to their original decision to participate in the Minister's Committee and to continue to press for recognition of the CSW as the body to represent women's organisations.

On 20 December 1974 the Minister announced the establishment of the Women's Representative Committee and the appointment of the members as follows: chairwoman : Mrs Eileen Desmond, TD; nominated by ICTU: Nabla McGinly, Derry McDermot, Joan O'Connell, Peter Cassells; nominated by FUE : Michael Hennigan, C E Hilliard (later replaced by Joe Colgan), John Dunne, Deirdre Murphy; CSW: Monica Barnes, Dr Hazel Boland, Hilda Tweedy; ESRI: Kathleen O'Higgins, Minister for Labour: Yvonne Murphy. Meetings were held at the Department of Labour and Elizabeth Murphy of the department was secretary.

The Women's Representative Committee, (WRC), met regularly with the Minister to discuss subjects which we had examined at his suggestion, as well as memoranda of our own. The WRC met various women's organisations to discuss submissions they had made. It undertook the running of the National Women's Talent Bank which was originally set up by the BPW to supply a comprehensive list of women suitable to serve on state and semi-state bodies, Louie Somerville acting as honorary secretary. The Women's Political Association had started a list of their own, but later the two organisations arranged to work together.

During its term of office the WRC studied many subjects concerning women among which were the following: examination of training facilities available to women; the need for free legal aid and advice in family cases; discrimination against women in social security; the domicile of the married woman; the need for family planning legislation; examination of the law of nullity in Ireland.

I have dealt at some length with the WRC but it is relevant to the development of the work of the CSW and all its affiliates, as the organisations received regular reports and were deeply involved in gathering the information used in the work. For example the government sent two members of the WRC, Deirdre Murphy of FUE and myself, to attend the UN Conference to mark International Women's Year in Mexico. We were joined there by Mrs Carmel Heaney, then Irish Consul in Boston, where we shared the distinction with Iceland of being the only two nations represented entirely by women. This was a tremendous learning experience and we brought back information which was useful, not only to the government and the WRC, but also to the CSW and the IHA.

After working with the WRC on its memorandum on family planning legislation, the CSW decided that it should express some opinion on family planning and sent the following letter to affiliates on 6 March 1974 : 'It has been suggested since the last Council meeting that we should express an opinion on family planning as it is mentioned in the report. Do you think that the Council should write a letter to the press as drafted below - or that each organisation should be left to deal with this matter as it chooses?

'Draft letter on Family Planning:
'Bearing in mind the UN Proclamation of Human Rights in Teheran in 1968 that 'parents have a basic human right to determine freely and responsibly the number and spacing of their children' and that couples have the right to 'adequate education and information' in this respect, the Council for the Status of Women supports the recommendation on family planning contained in the Report of the National Commission on the Status of Women as below:

Paragraph 574 of Report.
' We recommend accordingly, that :
(1) Information and expert advice on family planning should be available through medical and other channels throughout the country. Such advice should respect the moral and personal attitudes of each married couple.
(2) Medical requirements arising out of the married couples' decisions on family planning should be available under control and through channels to be determined by the Department of Health.

We ask our legislators to bear these recommendations in

mind when voting on the issue of family planning.'

It should be remembered that one of the terms of reference of the Council for the Status of Women was 'To press for the implementation of the Report of the National Council on the Status of Women' and yet two years after our foundation the affiliates with just a few exceptions replied to the above letter saying that as there was no consensus amongst their members, their organisation could not express an opinion on family planning. The IHA also found itself in this position. The CSW decided that under the circumstances no statement could be made, each affiliate must deal with the matter separately.

Meanwhile the work of the CSW went on and during 1974 we started preparations for the United Nations International Women's Year to be held in 1975. Through the IHA affiliation with the International Alliance of Women we had access to the UN directives sent to national governments on steps to be taken to celebrate International Women's Year, as copies had been sent to all the NGOs.

The CSW studied the UN directive and decided that we would plan a two-day international seminar on the theme of Women's Year: 'Equality, Development and Peace', and ask the government to fund it.

The Minister for Labour, Mr O'Leary, had been given responsibility for International Women's Year in Ireland, so we presented him with the plan for the seminar and a programme of events planned by our affiliates to be held during 1975 throughout the country. The Minister received us sympathetically, but there were the usual delays about funding. Meanwhile we had to find the deposit to book the RDS as best we could. The Minister lent the CSW 500 pounds to run the seminar, and eventually he gave us the money, our first government grant, in recognition of the success of the seminar.

The seminar was held in the Concert Hall of the RDS on 2 and 3 February 1975, the Minister having given a reception for the speakers and guests at the National Gallery the night before. The Concert Hall was packed to capacity for each session of the seminar, with women from all over Ireland, including a large contingent from Northern Ireland.

The Taoiseach, Mr Liam Cosgrove, opened the seminar in the presence of the Minister for Labour, Mr O'Leary who also spoke. Six sessions were held :

Elimination of Discrimination against Women
Speakers: Mrs Rasil Basu, UN Secretariat for Women's Year; Dr Patrick Hillery, EEC Commissioner.

National Commission's Report on the Status of Women
Speakers: Dr Thekla Beere, Commission chair; Professor Michael Fogarty, Commission member.

United Nations Conventions
Speakers: Mrs Laurel Casinader, vice-president, IAW.

Sunday, 2 February 1975 began with an interdenominational service, the lessons and prayers were read by women of different denominations. The sessions that day were:

Women in politics.
Speakers: Dr Eva Kolstad, UN IWY secretariat; Mrs Eileen Desmond, TD.

Education for Living
Speakers: Mrs Betty Fahy, IFA; Mrs Joan Carmichael, ICTU; Mr Cecil A Bell, FUE; Mr Michael Murphy, AONTAS.

Women for Peace
Speakers: Senator Mary Robinson, Miss Sadie Patterson, Miss Claire McMahon, Dr Edith Loane and a guest appearance by Mr Seán McBride, Nobel Prize winner.

The seminar was a tremendous success. It brought women together, members of the various women's organisations. But perhaps more important, women belonging to no organisation had travelled long distances to attend.

We received letters from all over the country expressing appreciation of the seminar, but best of all was the feeling of achievement among the affiliates that we had managed to plan and carry through this big event on sheer woman power and determination with practically no financial backing. Not only did every delegate to the CSW work for this, but the members of the affiliated organisations worked in teams to help with all the preparations, saving money by delivering leaflets etc. No task was too little or too big for them to tackle. During the seminar itself the response of the members of the affiliates was

59

tremendous and this gave a great feeling of solidarity amongst the women involved.

Special mention must be made of three women who worked day and night on the project - Anne Kavanagh, then honorary secretary of CSW, Margaret Waugh, past honorary secretary, and Monica Barnes, PRO for the Council.

Throughout International Women's Year government departments, the affilates of CSW and other organisations carried out many events which were assisted by funding from the Department of Labour:

At the end of the year the work of CSW was known all over Ireland and also at the United Nations and in Europe. We had shown the government that we were a responsible determined body of women. The Minister's grant of 500 pounds was in recognition of this. However, after the euphoria and sense of elation of the seminar, we had still to wait a further three years for any significant recognition of the Council. This came in 1978 when the term of the Women's Representative Committee expired and Mr Gene Fitzgerald, then Minister for Labour, decided to set up the Employment Equality Agency (on which the CSW was then represented by Monica Barnes, Anne Kavanagh and myself), to deal with employment while the CSW were assigned the task of monitoring the implementation of the remaining recommendations of the report and the working of the talent bank.

The IHA, through its delegates, was deeply involved in the long struggle for recognition and funding for the Council and our members played an active part in its work.

Women in public life

The IHA had always been strictly non-party in politics and was most careful not to be branded in any way. We had a rule that if one of our officers was standing for a particular party, or was elected as the representative of any political party to government or local government, that person must resign from office in the Association. Otherwise members, of course, were free to belong to the party of their choice provided they did not introduce party political views into the IHA. This left us free to work with all the parties, and support their various policies when they fitted in with the views of the Association, or criticise them when they did not.

Thus we were able to endorse the candidature of Hannah Sheehy Skeffington when she stood as an Independent candidate sponsored by the Women's Social and Progressive League for the Dail in 1942, and some of our members helped in her campaign.

During her period of office as chairwoman Jean Coote stood for election as an Independent to Dublin Corporation in 1950, and we actively campaigned for her, canvassing for her in her area. Though narrowly defeated, Jean Coote gained wide support in many areas. We felt that if she had had the opportunity to stand at the next election, she would have had no difficulty in being elected, but sadly she died in 1953. The IHA lost a most enthusiastic chairwoman who did so much to train our members in procedure and public speaking.

Our next venture was in 1957 when at an Extraordinary General Meeting held on 13 February it was decided to nominate the following candidates for the general election : Miss Kathleen Swanton, who had worked for several years as assistant honorary secretary to the IHA; Mrs Beatrice Dixon, chairwoman, 1954/55, and who had served on the central committee for many years; Mrs Mairead McGuinness, joint honorary secretary.

This campaign was a great learning experience for the IHA

and shows what can be done with practically no money but with great enthusiasm. Since 1953 we had built up the nucleus of an election fund because for a long time we had ambitions about putting up Independent women candidates. This fund now stood at fifty-two pounds and one shilling. This was obviously inadequate, so we made appeals for money. Guarantees and subscriptions were given by our members and their friends, members of the public and manufacturing firms, some of whom we had opposed in the past. In this way we collected 489 pounds 11 shillings and 6 pence, the top subscription being a cheque for 100 pounds from the late Dr James Quin, who had acted as gynaecologist to some of us. So with total funds of 541 pounds 12 shillings 6 pence we nominated our candidates and paid deposits of 100 pounds each. We printed their literature and distributed it by hand while canvassing. We mobilised most of our members for this task. With the remainder of the money we hired a lorry and megaphone (no microphones for us). Members took turns to go on the lorry each evening. We stopped the lorry wherever we saw a few people together and addressed them through the megaphone, asking for support for our candidates.

Beatrice Dixon was eliminated at the seventh count in the Rathmines area, going down at the same count as Seán McBride, who had been a Minister in the previous government. Kathleen Swanton was eliminated at the second count in North Dublin, but her name became so well known that she had no difficulty in being elected to Dublin Corporation at the next local election, as an Independent ratepayer, put forward by a group of women, many of whom were IHA members. Mairéad McGuinness lost her deposit in the Howth area, but this was largely due to so few of our members living in that area. We felt that if we had concentrated our efforts on two candidates we would probably have had both of them elected.

Although none of our candidates was elected we drew attention to the need for representation of women by women and the gross imbalance of the sexes in government. The experience built up a new solidarity among members, a determination to go on working for our various aims against all odds.

In 1966 the IHA sponsored our joint honorary secretary,

Carmel Gleeson, to stand as an Independent candidate for Dublin County Council in the Ballybrack/Stillorgan area. Once again our members and supporters rallied round and gave of their best, fund-raising and canvassing, and due to their efforts Carmel Gleeson was elected. Unfortunately for the IHA, who had to answer to our supporters, Carmel decided that she would be able to do more if she joined a political party, so she joined Fianna Fáil and shortly afterwards resigned from the IHA.

That was the last occasion the IHA put forward candidates of our own, but we continued to encourage women to seek nomination for the Dáil, Senate and Local Government and at each election wrote to the press asking for support for women candidates to redress the imbalance in representation, asking the electorate to vote for women where possible. We never advocated voting for women just because they were women, but because they had something to contribute. We firmly believed that there were sufficient qualified women in every political party to warrant more of them being nominated as candidates for election.

One of the more imaginative projects to highlight the need for more women in the Dáil was a Model Parliament organised by the international committee of the IHA on 12 November 1972.

In her opening address our Chairwoman, Betty Morrissey, stressed that the IHA was non-sectarian and non-party, the chief aim being to gain women's right to play an active part in all spheres of planning for the community. This emphasised women's right to be elected to decision-making positions in the Dáil. Beatrice Dixon acted as Ceann Comhairle and before opening proceedings she explained that this was a Model Parliament, not a Mock Parliament, to show that women could act out the proceedings of parliament with dignity and courtesy, following the procedures of Standing Orders as far as possible.

After opening the session with a reading from the Old Testament the 'Ceann Comhairle' called on the 'Minister for Justice', Catherine McGuinness, to open the committee stage of a Bill to amend the Constitution of Ireland. The 'Minister for Justice' said no constitution could make ideal citizens but it could prevent discrimination and injustice and should guarantee the maximum degree of equality and liberty for all citizens without imposing the moral conscience of one section of the community on all others.

The 'Minister' introduced the first amendment to alter Article 16 to allow votes at the age of eighteen. People of eighteen earned their living and paid taxes and should have the right to vote. Referring to Article 40, section 6, sub-section 1, which deals with press censorship, she said that this section could excuse over - repressive moral censorship and government interference with the media on political grounds and needed to be amended.

The 'Minister' asked for deletion of Article 41, section 2, as it is symbolic of male dominated society to subservient woman, stressing her duties in the home rather than her rights as a person. The married woman working in the home has no legal or economic identity. Mrs McGuinness amended Article 41, section 3, by deletion of the words from 'and protect it from attack'. She said the constitutional prohibition of any law on divorce was an example of the tendency to denominational legislation. All churches have moral laws binding on their members to obey. It was time to recognise that there were marriage failures and take steps to deal with the social consequences.

In Article 44, section 1, the 'Minister' suggested the deletion of sub-sections 2 and 3. The Constitution already guarantees freedom of conscience and religion. Mrs McGuinness added an article to the Constitution which stated :' The European Convention for the Protection of Human Rights and Fundamental Freedoms as agreed at Rome on 4 November,1950, shall be included as an integral part of the Constitution of Ireland, and shall have the same legal force as all other provisions of this Constitution.'

Míne Cribben, acting as Shadow Minister for Justice for the 'Opposition', said the Constitution was designed for the Irish people, and she saw no reason for changing it, but would consider changes if Northern Ireland was to join the Irish Republic. On votes at eighteen, she would rather suggest twenty-five as violence is more prevalent among the 18-21 age group. Young people were very immature she said.

On divorce she stressed that under the Constitution no one is deprived of the means of following their own conscience. Referring to the amendment on press censorship Mrs Cribben said a democracy must not allow the infiltration of elements which could destroy that democracy.

On Article 44 Mrs Cribben stated that the Catholic Church did not claim the right to make laws for the country. The fact that the Church's place was enshrined in the Constitution was that it was recognised as the expression of the majority of the people. Catholics had contracted to obey the laws of State and the law of the Pope.

Nuala Fennell, as 'Minister for Finance', introduced an interim budget to eliminate financial discrimination against women. The 'Minister' said 'Our country has, for too many generations, paid lip service to a Constitution that seems to elevate the position of the family and the status of the mother to untold heights. The family, which is the very kernel of the community, is safeguarded and harmonious only when everything is going well: but if misfortune, in the shape of death, marital break-down, unemployment or poverty, intervenes, mothers and their children suffer more than anyone should have to do. Our people, through their elected governments, in the past, have tolerated a system which penalises the unfortunate citizens, with the excuse that we are a poor nation, and cannot afford the standard of social welfare befitting a country which very proudly terms itself Christian, while at the same time we turn a blind eye to the activities of the speculators and other get-rich-quick-at-any-cost merchants. Instead of saying we cannot afford to fight poverty, we should realise that we can no longer afford not to fight it.'

Nuala Fennell stated that increased funds from the newly imposed VAT could be used to help finance the changes she proposed, such as: children's and family allowances, in the case of married couples, would in future be paid to the wife; children's allowance would be raised to two pounds per week for every child after the first, be continued to the age of sixteen unless the child was at full time college or school, when it would be continued until nineteen; a means test would be imposed restricting payment to families with yearly income of less than £3000; differences in payments between contributory and non-contributory pensions to widows would cease; allowances to widows and deserted wives would be standardised at eight pounds per week, no means test would be imposed for children's allowances in this section; a State Life Insurance would be introduced for all married male workers under sixty five, benefits of £1000 to be paid to the widow on production of the death certificate, free of estate duty.

On income tax married women would get income relief of one quarter of income, up to a maximum of £500 per annum: increased personal allowance to £104 to equate it with that of two single persons: housekeeper allowance of £100 where there were children.

On equal pay for equal work the 'Minister' proposed that the recommendations of the Interim Report on Equal Pay of the National Commission on the Status of Women be fully implemented.

Mrs Jenny Gilbert, BL,'Shadow Minister for the Opposition', welcomed long overdue increases in children's allowances. She spoke at length on social problems and advocated increased tax on drink and tobacco to cover the cost of health services caused by them. She suggested that the 'Minister' should provide creches for the children of working mothers. Mrs Gilbert welcomed the proposals for widows and deserted wives and the changes in income tax allowances, but felt that the compulsory saving scheme would place too heavy a burden on low income earnings. She agreed with the recommendations on equal pay for equal work.

Rev Mother Jordana, OP, 'Minister for Education' introduced a bill on community schools, explaining that this would provide for equality of opportunity. A wide range of subjects would be available; each would discover his or her abilities. Mother Jordana saw the community school as serving new areas where they would become pacemakers in community education. Community schools could become an extension of first level education; the best in secondary and vocational education should be combined. Those who drop out of education at an early age should be encouraged to return and develop latent talents, so that they can lead happier lives and contribute more to the society in which they live. The 'Minister' stated that the structure of community schools would be: a board of management to include post primary agencies, parents, members of the community and teachers; all teaching posts would be advertised and teachers chosen by professionals; the community schools would be non-denominational and open to all.

Miss Rosaleen Mills, welcoming the bill, said that this is a non-party matter and should have been worked out by an all-party committee. She congratulated the 'Minister' on the concept but wondered would the introduction of community schools mean the closing of more small country schools. She was filled with horror at the thought of long journeys twice daily for children. Nursery schools were needed, she said; these would be a tremendous help to mothers living in housing estates and blocks of flats. Young people were beginning to opt out. How can we reach them? It is important they continue at school. The future of our country is in the hands of the young. We must be careful what they learn. We are offering them votes at eighteen.

The members of the audience acted as TDs and joined in the debate which was lively; many interesting interventions were made. The Model Parliament got excellent press coverage and part of it was re-enacted on *The Late, Late Show*. It certainly focused attention on the part women could play in legislation and the IHA was congratulated on its success.

It is interesting now as a document on the social history of the time and to see how much we have progressed in the last twenty years. Some of the problems are still very much with us.

Membership and branches

At first the membership of the IHA was built up by word of mouth. Members invited small groups of friends to their homes, members of the committee spoke to them about the work of the IHA, and so people joined. The press helped greatly by printing our letters and reporting various events. Women marching in the streets was news at that time !

In the spring of 1947 our first branch was formed in Dun Laoghaire with Diana Buchanan as honorary secretary. In 1948 branches were formed in New Ross and Mount Merrion and in 1949 in Skerries, Bray and Dundrum. The IHA was growing, we were doing well, but trouble lay ahead.

On 6 April 1949 the IHA received a circular letter from the British Cultural Committee for Peace. This letter was sent to several organisations in Ireland, inviting them to send a peace message to a World Congress for Peace to be held in Paris. The letter was read to a general meeting and it was unanimously agreed to send a message, to be drafted by the central committee, and it was put on the agenda for the following meeting, branch secretaries being notified. After a full discussion on the wisdom of sending any message to a congress some of whose sponsors might suggest communism, the majority, (nine to three, Andreé Skeffington dissenting), voted to send the following carefully prepared message: 'We, the Irish Housewives Association, being an organisation independent of all political parties, call on the women of the world to sink their political differences and unite to work for peace. We welcome any genuine efforts to preserve peace, and believe that the women of the world, like ourselves, desire peace to bring up their children in a free country, where freedom from want, freedom of religion, freedom of speech and the civil liberties of the individual are guaranteed.' This message, which could not be construed, by any stretch of imagination, to be support of communism, was despatched to Paris on 16 April 1949, together with copies and covering letters to the press, and was reported to a general meeting of the IHA on 20 April. No complaints were received from any quarter. Our message was not printed in any paper when sent, but some ten days later there was a report of a speech by the then Dean of Canterbury headed *Red Dean of Canterbury Addresses Paris Peace Conference* and underneath another headline *Irish Housewives Association sends message to Paris Peace Conference*, stating that we had sent a message, but not printing the text. Immediately we had complaints from our members and particularly from the Bray and Mount Merrion branches, and a special meeting was called on 18 May 1949 to discuss the whole matter. It was agreed by a large majority to send the following statement to the press: 'As our action in sending a message to the Paris Peace Congress has been misunderstood by some of our members and branches (protests were received from some of our Branches including Bray and Mount Merrion), and it appears to be misconstrued by some of the public, we wish to state that our message meant no more than it said, and we deny that it could possibly be taken as implying support of communism. It does not, of course, bind us in any way to acknowledge, or accept, any decisions made, or resolutions passed, by the Paris Congress. We ask fairminded people to re-read our message of peace demanding freedom of religion, freedom of speech and civil liberties for the individual, and to note that it could in no sense be taken as a pro-communist message.'

This statement was sent to all the Dublin daily papers and to the Catholic Weekly paper, *The Standard*, and was published in the *Irish Press* (24 May), and the *Evening Mail* (10 June). Meanwhile *The Standard* had published a highly inaccurate report of the Mount Merrion and Bray protests under the heading *Message to Reds splits Housewives Association*. We wrote to *The Standard* sending the original statement and correcting major errors of fact in their report, requesting the editor to publish the corrections, but this he failed to do. The Bray branch had resigned unanimously on 6 May and finally, at an extraordinary meeting on 30 May 1949, the Mount Merrion branch (membership 146), decided, by a majority of twenty to thirteen, to dissolve the branch.

This was a major set-back for our membership, as individual members also resigned. It indicates the fear of communism at the time and the damage which could be done to an organisation by the mere suggestion of having anything to do with such politics. Unfortunately the IHA had been branded, entirely unjustifiably, but this was used against us on more than one occasion by those who did not agree with some aspects of our work.

In 1950 our attention was drawn to an article headed, *'An informal amd factual article proving there is Communism - but disguised- in Eire!'* published in *Cavalcade*. The Irish Housewives Association was mentioned in it, along with other organisations, as being a communist-dominated organisation. The IHA took legal action on this libel and on receiving a letter from our solicitor, *Cavalcade* and the author of the article agreed to withdraw, without reservation, the statements made as having no foundation. An apology was printed in the paper.

On 12 April 1952 the *Roscommon Herald* published an article under the heading of *Dangerous Trends in Ireland* in which it was suggested that the IHA had been mixed up with rioting in O'Connell Street, and that it had 'always been used as a medium of expression' by Marxists, communists or fellow-travellers. The committee was unanimous in deciding to place the matter with our solicitors who advised us that the article was defamatory. An apology and complete withdrawal was demanded on our behalf. The *Roscommon Herald* offered a totally unacceptable apology and our solicitors advised us to issue a writ for libel which was done in October 1952.

The IHA (represented by Mary Andrews and Andreé Skeffington), were actually in court waiting for the case to be heard on 28 July 1953 when the *Roscommon Herald* withdrew and the case was settled out of court. The *Roscommon Herald* agreed to publish an apology, pay legal costs on both sides, and a token sum of fifty pounds to the IHA.

Finally on 15 August 1953 the *Roscommon Herald* printed the following apology: 'In our issue of 12 April 1952, we published an article entitled *Dangerous Trends in Ireland* in the course of which it was stated: "For instance, the Irish Housewives Association is one body that, although its

70

membership is largely made up of people who have no Red sympathies, has always been used as a medium of expression by others whose ideological allegiance is not in doubt. And, as we expected, the Irish Housewives Association has been very much to the fore in voicing 'popular indignation' during the past week.(The IHA had protested at the rise in the cost of living due to the removal of food subsidies.) It is a mistake to play into the hands of these people. Governments can be removed by popular vote in this country. The government of Russia cannot be thus removed and if a crowd assembled in the Red Square in Moscow to demonstrate against Stalin's budget we know what would happen to them." We have now satisfied ourselves that there is no foundation whatever for this allegation, that the Irish Housewives Association has no connection whatever with any form of communism, and that it is not being used, nor has it at any time been used, as a medium of expression by persons being either communists, or persons with communist sympathies. We express our regret to the Association for the statement in question and agree to indemnify its committee against all legal costs and expenses incurred by them in connection with the publication complained of.'

These continuous erroneous allegations of communism, or of communist leanings, were extremely upsetting and disruptive for our members, especially in the climate of the time. Not only did it frighten many of our members, but also their husbands who feared that their livelihoods might be affected. This led to resignations and much turmoil in the Association.

Much of the opposition came from new members, including some from the newly constituted 'group members', who could join at a special rate of one shilling per head. In the weeks following the issuing of the writ in October 1952 an unusual influx of new members aroused the suspicion of the committee. On the advice of our solicitor in January 1953 a decision was taken to close the membership books temporarily, until the AGM in June, as it was thought some of the recruitment was being carried out unfairly.

Some of the members, including myself, opposed the taking of the libel action and the closing of the books on the grounds that the committee had acted without consulting the members. Three extraordinary meetings were requested by members during the year: (i) to amend the Constitution of the IHA; this was held on 25 June 1952 to consider seven proposed amendments (only one, to raise the annual subscription, was passed); (ii) to explain the action being taken against the *Roscommon Herald*; after explanation the committee's decision concerning the action against the *Roscommon Herald* was ratified by the extraordinary general meeting held in December 1952. (It certainly was the right decision to take because after the publication of the apology in the *Roscommon Herald* the media were careful not to libel us again in this manner.) (iii) to reverse the committee's decision to close the membership books. This request was not granted by the committee, since according to our Constitution no meeting other than the AGM could reverse a committee decision.

It is surprising that our support of Noel Browne's 'Mother and Child Scheme ' during that period of turmoil did not draw us into further trouble, at least not openly.

On 7 March 1951 Dr Noel Browne, Minister for Health, released the details of the 'Mother and Child Scheme', which stirred up so much controversy at the time, culminating in the resignation of the Minister. Today people cannot imagine how a plan to improve the health and welfare of the women and children of Ireland and which would be open to all, could possibly be so controversial.

The provisions of the Mother and Child Scheme were discussed at a general meeting of the IHA on 21 March 1951 and a resolution of support for the scheme was passed unanimously and the committee sent a letter to the press to that effect. It was printed in the *Evening Mail* on 5 April 1951.

Meanwhile Dr Noel Browne had run into opposition because there was no provision for a means test in the scheme from some members of the medical profession, who feared for their livelihood. More serious, however, were the views of the hierarchy of the Roman Catholic Church, as conveyed in a long letter from His Grace, Dr John McQuaid, Archbishop of Dublin, to the Taoiseach, Mr John Costello, dated 5 April 1951, in which it was stated : 'The Archbishops and Bishops desire to express once again approval of a sane and legitimate health service, which will properly safe-guard the health of mothers and children.

'The hierarchy cannot approve of any scheme which, in its general tendency, must foster undue control by the state in a sphere so delicate and so intimately concerned with morals as that which deals with gynaecology or obstetrics and with the relations between doctor and patient.

'Neither can the bishops approve of any scheme which must have for practical result the undue lessening of the proper initiative of individuals and associations and the undermining of self-reliance.'

The committee of the IHA met on 11 April, when the resignation of Dr Browne as Minister for Health was impending, and the following resolution was passed unanimously: 'We, the Committee of the IHA, affirm our belief that the principle of equal opportunities, enshrined in our Constitution, should be applied in the sphere of health to those least able to fend for themselves: the mothers and children of Ireland. We consequently re-affirm our support of the Mother and Child Scheme as proposed by the Minister for Health.' This resolution was sent to An Taoiseach, Mr Costello, and to the Minister for Health, Dr Noel Browne.

In the IHA Report for the year 1950-51 we commented on the Mother and Child episode as follows: 'We feel sure that our members will agree that, although as a non-party, non-sectarian organisation, we cannot now take sides, yet we cannot but deplore the manner in which an issue vital to the health of the nation was handled. We re-affirm our belief in the equal rights of all Irish women to happy motherhood, and deplore the resignation of a Minister for Health who had done so much in his term of office for the health of the community'.

My own particular memory of this period was, somewhere along the line, being on the back of a lorry in College Green, Dublin, with the two assistant honorary secretaries of the IHA, Ruth Deale and Kathleen Swanton, all eager to show IHA support for the scheme. Dr Noel Browne was there and several other supporters and a considerable crowd of people. Every time the would-be speakers raised the megaphone, their words were drowned by the crowd singing 'Faith of our Fathers'! Whatever the pros and cons of the Mother and Child Scheme and the discussions and arguments to which it gave rise, the effects on the IHA were not nearly as devastating for us as the communist smear.

Meanwhile the work of the IHA went on. We had sent memoranda to the various governments on the cost of living, public health and food hygiene, emigration and population problems. We investigated the quality and quantity of the Dublin District Milk Supply and gave evidence at the Tribunal of Inquiry into the Dublin Milk Supply in April 1945. We also prepared memoranda and gave evidence at the public sittings of the Prices Advisory Body, set up in 1951 as a tribunal of arbitration between manufacturers, retailers and consumers. The IHA investigated the claims for increases in prices made by the manufacturers and retailers, on commodities such as tea, bacon, pork, turf, fish, meat, eggs and bread.

The IHA steadily built up a reputation for dedicated work on behalf of the consumer and particularly for women and children. This was recognised by the government and we may take some credit for the setting up of the Milk Tribunal, and of the Prices Advisory Body, both accepting written and verbal evidence from the consumer, a right which we used fully. The willingness of government departments to receive deputations and discuss our memoranda, and on occasions to consult us on aspects of our work and even to include some of our suggestions in legislation, eg in public health and food hygiene regulations was proof of the value of our work. We were fortunate to have so many women willing to give so much time to the work of the Association, often at considerable financial cost to themselves.

It is interesting that in the midst of the period when aspersions were being cast on the credentials of the IHA *The Standard* printed an appreciation of our work. Here are extracts from an article which appeared in *The Standard* on 9 March 1951 which gives an assessment of our work: 'The Irish Housewives Association was started less than a decade ago in an endeavour to assist and organise the housewife,"so long at the mercy of trade and till".'

'Today, as in 1941, threatened emergencies and falling supplies are producing those up and up prices that nullify wage increases and reduce those on fixed incomes to desperation. The Prices Advisory Body (PAB), sitting recently in Griffith Barracks to hear the application of the Dublin Coal Merchants' Association for a price of ten pounds, thirteen and eleven pence a ton for coal, would have had no opposition only for the unpaid representatives of the Housewives' Association and the Lower Prices Council. The members of those two groups do not also belong to the idle rich (if such exist today!), but are ordinary women with homes and families to cater for like ourselves. The chief difference is probably that they take an unusually wide and intelligent interest in public affairs, knowing that such have a powerful and intimate bearing on private matters.

'Since 1942 the IHA has worked untiringly for a campaign of education on cleaner handling of food and for the establishment of a minimum standard of hygiene in all food handling premises from farm or factory to kitchen, and it strove for a "long-range publicity campaign on such matters as hygiene and health" initiated by a Minister for Public Health. Much of our thanks for the new Food Hygiene Regulations which are bound to do so much towards protecting health are due to the Irish Housewives Association for their successful efforts towards that end... If its enthusiasm for its difficult and sometimes even unpopular, task should ever fail who, I wonder, would trouble to shoulder the burden?'

The years from 1948 to 1952 were a time of change and growth although there was some unrest in the IHA. Membership was increasing, branches were being formed, the scope of our work for the consumer was extending all the time, our interest in feminist issues was being actively pursued and our involvement with the International Alliance of Women was also taking more time and attention.

Up till 1950 there had not been much change in the IHA committee, although from 1942 to 1950 we had had three different chairwomen, Susan Manning, Marie Mortished and Jean Coote; Frances Scott and later, Maude Rooney, had replaced Betty Morrissey as honorary treasurer. Andrêe Skeffington and I had remained as joint honoray secretaries, and as the work increased, Ruth Deale and Mrs McGregor had been appointed as honorary assistant secretaries, the latter being replaced by Kathleen Swanton after one year.

Andrée and I had worked very closely for the first years, but as pressure of work from the various controversies mentioned above and the problems created by them, increased, difficulties arose. The time had come for change, so I decided to resign from the committee and as joint honorary secretary in December 1951 and concentrate on the work for the Lower Prices Council. Ruth Deale and Kathleen Swanton also resigned from the committee, but both continued to work for the Association in various other capacities. At this time we had our meeting place in South Leinster Street, and for a period of nine months had a paid part-time secretary which lightened the volume of work for the committee. This was the only time we were able to afford even part-time secretarial help.

The IHA suffered two serious losses soon after this, first by the death in March 1952 of our vice-chairwoman, Mrs Aine Heron, who had started our branch in Dundrum, and again in November 1953 when our chairwoman, Jean Coote, died. Both these women gave of their best to the IHA during a difficult period, as did Mary Andrews, who served as vice-chairman from 1953 to 1956. Great credit must go to them, and to Andrêe Skeffington, who guided and carried out the work of the Association at this time.

Unfortunately Andrêe Skeffington had not been well for some time after a major operation and could not attend meetings. With a growing feeling of alienation from the Association as a result of the trouble caused by the libel actions, she resigned as joint honorary secretary and from the committee in September 1955. Andrée Skeffington's resignation was a great loss to the IHA as she has not played an active part in the Association since then. Members who have joined since may not realise the debt that the IHA owes to her work in our formative years. It was she who initiated and built up our reputation for meticulous research into any project we undertook, which has stood to us over the

years, so that her name has been associated with us throughout
our history.

Branches

The Irish Housewives Association was never very successful
with its branches, although a few of them survived for several
years and did very good work. There were various reasons for
this lack of success, one being that the IHA was a pressure
group, and branches in towns, where everybody knew everyone,
had difficulty in making protests about over-charging or
unhygienic handling of food, without treading on the toes of
friends and relations. In some cases branches were set up and
built around personalities, and when for one reason or another,
these people were no longer able to work, it was difficult to
replace them. There was also the difficulty of finding suitable
premises, which had neither political or sectarian connotations,
an important consideration at that time. Another very potent
reason was that the IHA did not have the financial resources to
service the branches properly.

In 1947 our first branch was set up in Dun Laoghaire with
Diana Buchanan as honorary secretary. The branch dealt with
local issues such as the provision of a bicycle park, a general
clean-up campaign, the monitoring of cleanliness in shops and
dairies, and the display of price notices in shops. The branch was
represented on an IHA deputation to the Department of Health.
Lectures on various topics were organised as were some social
occasions, but it was difficult to find suitable premises for
meetings. In 1951 the branch decided that members could serve
the IHA better by joining the central body and attending
meetings in Dublin.

On 30 May 1968 this branch was reformed after the IHA held
a public meeting in Dun Laoghaire with Mrs Jane Carroll as
chairwoman. Mrs Carroll later became a valued member of the
central committee in Dublin. The branch again dealt with local
affairs such as the proposed new swimming pool and the
condition of public toilets as well as raising awareness regarding
hygiene and litter disposal. Members joined in the National Food
Hygiene Week and helped with price surveys and the survey of
packaged goods. Another campaign was for free turf and butter

for old age pensioners. In 1976 the branch reported a severe drop in membership as members became disheartened about the rise in the cost of living and, in spite of a membership drive, they decided to close the following year.

In 1948 four new branches were formed in Bray, Mount Merrion, New Ross and Skerries. As explained above, the Bray and Mount Merrion branches closed in 1949 over the *Roscommon Herald* libel issue. The Bray branch was not really established when this occurred but we were particularly sorry to lose the Mount Merrion branch which started well with 146 members under Eileeen Petrie as chair and had already done good work on the monitoring of prices and food hygiene, representing the IHA on a deputation to the Minister for Health, Dr Noel Browne. This was the first occasion we were received by a Minister. Many of the members joined the central branch and continued with us over the years. Among them was Eileen Petrie who has made such a practical contribution to our work.

The New Ross branch did useful work concerning social welfare, particularly as related to children, and also in the area of food hygiene. They explored the need for producer/consumer markets and campaigned for a public ambulance and a public playground. In 1950 the branch declined and faded out.

The Skerries branch took up the question of transport to the town and made submissions about the train and bus services. In 1950 Skerries decided not to work as a separate branch and some members joined the central branch.

In 1949 the Dundrum branch was formed and joined in the clean food and litter campaigns of the IHA, as well as local issues such as protests about the state of the footpaths, the collection of refuse in uncovered lorries, the increase in water rates. It campaigned for a public park and swimming pool and asked for a bank in the village. In 1953 the branch decided to dissolve and join the Dublin branch, bringing in many useful members, including Mrs Aine Heron, Mrs Barry, Mrs Hanna and Mrs Corboy, all of whom held office in various capacities in the IHA.

The Drogheda branch was formed in 1951 and flourished until 1974 due to the efforts of Mrs Clare Shaw Hamilton, Mrs

Catherine Smyth, Mrs Moira Cocoran and Mrs Gretta Holden, the latter two serving as honorary secretaries for several years. The branch took up health issues, such as tuberculosis, its treatment and prevention, diphtheria immunisation, foot ailments, the care of children's teeth and eyes, conditions in the local dispensary and the collection of refuse. The branch supported the various campaigns of the IHA, such as the anti-litter campaign, Buy Irish campaign, National Hygiene Week. Its members helped in price surveys, and organised local boycotts during the 'War on Prices'. Drogheda members joined in our twenty-first anniversary celebrations and helped to organise the visit of delegates to the IAW congress in 1961, to the Medical Missionaries of Mary Hospital in Drogheda. The Drogheda branch ran lectures on many different subjects of public interest and organised social and fund-raising activities, the proceeds of which helped to supply coal to old age pensioners and the needy. The IHA was disappointed to lose this branch in 1974 when interest declined after twenty three years of very useful work.

The Cork branch was formed in November 1951, Andreé Skeffington and Aine Heron travelling to Cork to open it. The branch was received by the Minister for Agriculture on 16 February 1952 to hear the consumer's side when the milk producers demanded an increase in prices and later that afternoon members held a public meeting to protest against the milk producers' campaign. On 25 February a deputation from the branch was received by the Lord Mayor and this led to a full corporation debate on the price and distribution of milk in the Cork area, resulting in support for the branch's claims. This was a first successful year in which the membership rose to 224. During the period from 1952 to 1958 the Cork branch was very active, with Mrs May Brennan as honorary secretary. It carried out many investigations such as: the meat content in sausages, the profit on sale of wallpaper, the revision of bus fares (and succeeded in the fares being reduced in some areas), the supply and price of vegetables, bacon prices, gas, turf briquettes, fish (attended Prices Advisory Body inquiry and later organised a boycott of fish until prices were reduced). The branch also played an active part during the outbreak of polio in Cork. In

1959 the Cork branch closed down as it had not complied with our Constitution regarding public statements on policy.

In September 1965 the Cork branch was reformed with Mrs Collins in the chair after consultation with, and a visit from the executive of the central committee, who later attended the inaugural meeting to which the Lord Mayor and Lady Mayoress were invited, and many members of the former branch rejoined. The Cork branch worked actively on local issues such as bread deliveries, free fuel deliveries, litter, youth clubs, provision of seating in dispensaries, high price of poor quality coal, poor quality dirty potatoes, broken footpaths, bus fares and service, home holidays, consumer education, hygiene in Cork fish market. The branch supported all the IHA projects and carried out price surveys and joined in National Hygiene Week. In 1977 Cork reported a decline in attendance at meetings but continued work on litter and organised a march to protest at rising prices. They sent a letter of protest to the Lord Mayor who said he would convey their grievances to the appropriate government departments. We were disappointed that in the following year interest seemed to decline and the Cork branch faded out. During the period 1965 to 1978 Mrs Ita O'Connell served as chairwoman, and as honorary secretary, and the IHA is grateful to her and her committee for their work.

The Limerick branch was formed in May 1966 at a meeting attended by Mrs Rooney, Mrs Johnston and Mrs Bayly from the central commmittee and Mrs Collins and Mrs Cooke from the Cork branch. The branch worked on local issues such as clean milk, condition of public toilets and lack of toilets for women, and investigated prices of various commodities, including increase in rates. Members campaigned for improved dental services, better communication between parents and teachers, an 'emergency night service' to cope with sudden illness, and enforcement of Retail Price Display Order. The branch was represented on the Social Services Consultative Council and worked with the Ratepayers Association on a litter campaign. In 1970 after a talk by Mrs Liddy of the Limerick University committee the branch pledged its support for the planning committee. Besides supporting local events like the Limerick

Civic Week, the branch supported all IHA projects such as 'War on Prices' and National Hygiene Week. Members also helped with price surveys. Attendance declined from 1979 but the branch continued to hold lectures and social events until 1981 and a small group, although not active, continued to pay an affiliation fee for some years afterwards.

The Cavan branch was formed in April 1966 at a meeting attended by Maude Rooney, Kathleen Clarke, Carmel Gleeson and Nora Browne from the central commmittee who spoke on the aims of the IHA and our work. The first three years were an uphill struggle as attendance at meetings was poor, the programme consisting of cookery demonstrations and some talks. In 1970 Nora Browne, as national chairwoman, and other members of the central commmittee, attended a meeting at which the Cavan branch was reformed.

The central commmittee members spoke on the plans for National Hygiene Week and gave an account of the IAW congress which they had attended in Germany. The branch obtained the backing of the local health authority for National Hygiene Week and arranged a programme for Cavan.

Other interests were the monitoring of prices, the quality of goods, the effect of enzymes in washing powders, the introduction of decimal currency, the turnover tax and the enforcement of the Prices Display Order. The Cavan branch struggled on until 1974 despite poor attendance, and then closed having decided that the women in Cavan did not have time for voluntary organisations.

In 1972 four branches were formed under the guidance of Nora Browne as branches secretary: The Athlone branch was formed in June 1972 due to the efforts of Mrs Cousins who had joined the IHA the previous year. She was elected chairwoman. The branch got off to a good start with forty-one paid-up members and immediately dealt with several local issues and lodged complaints with bodies such as Athlone Urban District Council in connection with public health - refuse bins not collected; cars and lorries on the footpath; the provision of pedestrian crossings, particularly near schools. Letters were written to the Department of Industry and Commerce reporting failure to display price lists in shops and instances of over-charging. An inspector was sent down to check on these. The branch established contact with the local branches of ANCO, the Junior Chamber of Commerce and the credit unions. A series of lectures and demonstrations were arranged as well as social events. However, in 1974 interest waned and the branch closed down.

In April 1972 the IHA organised a public meeting in Naas with the help of Mrs Betty Fahy, seventeen members from Dublin attending. It was decided to form a branch with Mrs Gertrude Jeffers as chairman and thiry-one women joined. The branch took up the question of teenage drinking and passed a motion deploring 'drink advertising aimed at the upper teenage and early twenties age group, who are usually learning to drive at this age'. The branch arranged several public meetings in Naas with speakers, some from the IHA, on the National Prices Commission, ecology, the farming community, the running of a supermarket, and practical demonstrations of commodities were held. The public meetings were well attended, and members from Drogheda and Dublin attended on occasions. It is difficult to understand why interest seemed to die in 1975 when the branch faded out.

The Carlow branch was formed in November 1972 at a meeting at which Nora Browne and members of the central commmittee spoke. Mrs Ina Broughall (a member of the ICA who later became its president) was elected chairwoman. Meetings were held and Mr Kevin O'Regan from the Regional College spoke on the metric system. In spite of a good start the branch did not survive the year.

The Dundalk branch was inaugurated in May 1972 at a large meeting attended by Nora Browne as national chairwoman, Gretta Morrison, Molly Cranny, Mairéad Allen and Kay Daly from the central commmittee who spoke on different aspects of our work, followed by a lively question time.

The women present felt there was a need for a branch of the IHA in Dundalk and agreed to form it. Mrs Bridie O'Rourke was elected chairwoman. The branch took action on various local issues, invited local authorities to speak on specific subjects such as litter; the cooking of cheaper cuts of meat with a demonstration of the different cuts by a local butcher; the disappearance of the halfpenny coin (prices being rounded upwards); the Malicious Injury Claims being added to the rates. The branch pressed for the appointment of a prices inspector for Dundalk and pointed out that there was only one health inspector for all purposes in the area. The branch was invited to nominate two members to work on a local representative committee to promote local industry and the purchase of Irish goods. The branch also organised help for elderly and handicapped people. It took part in the National Prices Survey in conjunction with the IHA and RTE. Members entertained four women from the Deutscher Frauenring, who were visiting the IHA. The Dundalk and Drogheda branches exchanged visits and found this helped their work. They also organised peace events with other interested bodies. In 1977 the branch reported that it had only twelve paid-up members. Public meetings were well attended but women did not join, so the branch closed. This was a disappointment as members of the Dundalk branch appeared to be very enthusiastic and assiduous in attending branch meetings and the AGM of the Association in Dublin.

In 1974 three branches were formed, although two of these, in Arklow and Youghal, did not survive the first year. After our protest march against rising prices in Dublin, the Arklow branch held its own march locally.

The Ennis branch, inaugurated by Nora Browne in April 1974, was more successful. With Mrs Griffin as chairwoman a series of meetings were arranged on: Hygiene in shops and in the home; price differentials in supermarkets; dangers of drug abuse; women's rights; women in political life. Contact was made with the Chamber of Commerce to point out how anxious housewives were about the high prices in Ennis, forcing them to shop in other towns. The branch joined with the Chamber to picket a 'sale of the century' organised by outside traders as being against community interests. A 'weekly shopping basket' survey was undertaken to monitor prices. In December 1975 the Ennis branch organised a peace march to coincide with a peace march in Dublin, but this was poorly attended. They arranged a meeting on 'battered babies'. As a gesture to International Women's Year it was suggested that two members should be nominated to sit on the Chamber of Commerce. This was agreed by the Chamber and Mrs Delia Griffin and Mrs Mary Kenny were accepted. In 1978 the branch became involved in community development and worked with other organisations such as the Tidy Towns Organisation, Bord Fáilte, An Taisce, the ICA and the Archaeological and Historical Society. After that the interest in the IHA waned and the branch faded away.

This is a short account of the branches. It is not possible to list all the work done or all the people involved. Although some only survived for a short time the IHA gained new members, quite a few of whom remained after the particular branch might have closed, and people in the country became aware of our work. It was difficult to maintain continuous contact with the branches because of our slender resources and some felt that the IHA was too Dublin-orientated. The Dublin committee was the central commmittee of the IHA and each branch could nominate a member to it. Special branch meetings were organised regularly, but here again lack of funds prevented branch members travelling. A branches secretary was appointed to keep in touch and send information regularly. Nora Browne and after her, Pat Davys, put a great deal of effort into this job. The IHA has always been grateful to the various branches for the work they did.

Women of action

The IHA has been fortunate to have had a succession of quite remarkable women who have been willing to use their talents in working for the Association with no material gain to themselves and indeed little recognition for the work they have done. We have never had a large membership. A little over 1200 was the most we ever reached, but we have acted as a very effective pressure group. From the beginning we wrote to the press on consumer issues, and anything affecting the health or welfare of women and children; we took part in radio and television programmes; we wrote to government ministers, sent memoranda to them and deputations to discuss the points we raised; we gave evidence at the sittings of the Prices Advisory Body, the Milk Tribunal and the Restrictive Practices Body; and we had representatives on various bodies set up by the government. To carry out this work effectively and efficiently we needed a team of researchers to do the back-up work.

It is always invidious to pick out individuals when so many people have given so much to the Association, but certain members have made outstanding contributions. Edith Cellem, who had been a teacher with the London County Council, came to live in Ireland and joined the IHA in the late '40s and immediately became involved in the research required for the evidence at the Prices Advisory Body, and in the preparation of various memoranda, eg education and emigration. She was also a hard-working member of the editorial board, as contributor and secretary for many years. Edith served as joint honorary secretary of the Association from 1957-1959.

As the membership grew various sub-committees were set up, and we claimed that no matter what the talents or tastes of our members were, they could find an outlet for them in the IHA through the sub-committees. The social and propaganda sub-committee was set up in October 1943 and for the fifty years of our existence has been responsible for organising social and fund-raising events and membership drives and it is due to the work of this committee that the IHA has managed to remain financially viable. It organised jumble sales, whist drives and concerts, our outings and annual dinners, receptions for the following: Madame Pandit, during her term as Indian ambassador to Ireland; for Dr Edith Summerskill, for the many occasions when the IAW presidents or board members visited Ireland, notably Dame Margaret Corbett-Ashby, Ester Graff, Olive Bloomer, Laurel Casinader, Amy Bush, Eva Kolstad, Brigitte Pross, as well as our friends from the Deutscher Frauenring in Kronberg with whom we exchange visits.(Our link with the Deutscher Frauenring came through IAW and has been a valuable contact which has given us great pleasure.)

Mary Meagher was a dedicated worker for the IHA and a wonderful organiser, a quiet woman with a sense of humour, who inspired her band of workers with a deep sense of loyalty, so that they never let her down, and were willing to turn their hands to anything. She formed a most successful work party, which met weekly to make goods to sell at the annual sale of work. Mary did a wonderful job during the IAW Congress when she organised the cafeteria for the delegates. Mary Meagher was also an active member of the central committee until her sudden death in 1967.

The social committee attracted a continuous band of dedicated women right down to the present day. Unfortunately it is not possible to mention all of them here, but some names must be recorded.

Isobel McDowell was one of the earliest and set a standard of hard work and initiative. Ida Kent was particularly successful in attracting new members and persuading her friends to attend our fund-raising efforts. She and her husband left to live in Canada in 1956 and very soon we had reports of her involvement in community projects there. Josephine Sheehan acted as honorary secretary of the social committee from 1967 to 1971 as well as taking part in the central committee. She was in charge of our premises and the premises committee. Members will remember her sitting at the door as they entered meetings, always ready with information or to take a subscription. May Duff, Margaret

McPartlin, Bridie Kelly, Nora Looney, May Cairns and Maureen Curran also worked on this committee, as well as in other areas of the IHA. Without their dedication we could not have survived.

No account of the social committee, or indeed, of the IHA, would be complete without mention of Abigail Cassidy. Abbie has worked on the social committee since she joined the Association. She and her daughter, Philomena Corcoran, are its mainstay today, still willing to organise and carry on the work. Abbie has served the IHA in many capacities and has worked on most of our committees. She has served several terms on the central committee, being honorary treasurer for 1966-1969 and joint honorary secretary for 1984-1986. Abbie Cassidy has represented the IHA on various bodies and at seminars and meetings organised by other groups. She has given a life-time of service. Abbie is a long standing member of the international committee and treasurer of that committee for several years, and has attended IAW congresses in Trieste, London, Konigstein and New York as an IHA delegate.

In 1951 the public relations committee, organised by Ruth Deale, was set up to publicise the IHA and increase membership. This committee carried out intensive canvassing campaigns in the Phibsboro' and Dun Laoghaire areas, ending in public meetings in these areas, gaining forty-three new members. During its year of work, twelve lectures, demonstrations or debates, were arranged and the first of our annual flag days organised.

In 1955 the publicity sub-committee was reformed with Mary Keane in charge and organised a most successful 'Housewives Week' in 1956 which included a press conference, cookery competition, children's art competition and a dinner attended by over 200 members and friends. The publicity and social committees always worked in close collaboration. Among others who worked on this committee were Nora Browne, Eileen Hackett, Lillie O'Callaghan, Marie Murray and Peggy Browning.

The international sub-committee was set up when the Irish Women Citizens Association joined the IHA in 1947 to deal with our affilation to the International Alliance of Women. It monitored family law and worked to raise the status of women in

87

Ireland. This subsequently led to the IHA involvement with the *Ad Hoc* committee on the Status of Women, which asked the government to set up the National Commission of Women in 1970, and in the formation of the Council for the Status of Women in 1972.

The international committee attracted members who were interested in the United Nations, women's rights and travel. Sheila Kennedy has been chairwoman of this committee for several years and has represented the IHA at IAW congresses in several countries as well being IHA delegate to the CSW. Sheila has also served as vice-chairwoman, honorary treasurer and joint honorary secretary of the IHA for two terms and has been a member of both editorial boards.

The late Dot Lloyd was a most enthusiastic member of the international committee. She was sent to us by Ezlynn Deranyagala who was a personal friend of hers in Sri Lanka. She also knew Ester Graff, another IAW president, through her connection with Unilever. Dot had worked with Unilever where she met her husband, Joe, and they happily travelled the world together, until they finally settled in Ireland. Dot also worked on both editorial boards and wrote many articles for the magazines on her travels. She represented the IHA on the UNICEF greetings card committee in Dublin.

The IHA has been represented on the Irish UNICEF committee since it was set up and two other members of the IHA have given distinguished service to UNICEF. Kitty Clarke, who has recently celebrated her ninetieth birthday, still keeps up her interest in UNICEF, and has represented that organisation abroad. Kitty was joint honorary secretary of the IHA from 1964-1967 and for many years a popular chairwoman of the social committee. Betty Hamilton also made her mark with the UNICEF committee and is not forgotten there, although ill-health now prevents her attending meetings. Betty Hamilton was our honorary treasurer from 1960 to 1963, and she was a valued member of the editorial board. She taught us many skills in editing and production as she had worked with a publisher in England before her marriage.

The IHA produced the first of its yearly magazines, *The Irish*

Housewife in 1946, through the initiative of Andrée Skeffington, and continued production until 1966. The work on the magazine was carried out by an editorial board, which approached people to write articles on subjects connected with our work. We are proud that so many prominent people considered it worth while to write for us, politicians, doctors, lawyers, teachers, authors and journalists, all without any financial reward. The editorial board was responsible, not only for the planning and contents of the magazine and the proof-correcting, but also for the actual design and lay-out. The magazine was published by the IHA in conjunction with an advertising agency who agreed to print a number of copies in return for the advertising revenue while the IHA had the proceeds of sales. We always kept control of the advertising and on occasions refused advertisements from firms who did not comply with the IHA standard for goods or services. As well as selling the magazine to our members, and distribution to the shops, the IHA took and managed, a stall at the RDS for the Spring Show and Horse Show to sell the *The Irish Housewife*, distribute information about the Association and recruit members.

In 1967, after our Silver Jubilee, we ceased publication of *The Irish Housewife* as it became very difficult to obtain advertisements although it sold reasonably well in the shops. We had to face the fact that television had superseded all other forms of advertising, and as there was a considerable drop in our revenue from this source, the magazine was no longer financially viable. Unfortunately, with its limited resources the IHA was unable to subsidise the work of the sub-committees; each had to be self-supporting. The closure of *The Irish Housewife* was a loss to the IHA, both as a source of income, since the magazine never failed to pay for itself and contribute to the funds of the Association, and as a vehicle to publicise our work.

The editorial board worked on until 1970, exploring means of filling the gap. We approached various established women's magazines with the idea of providing an IHA page once a month to provide our news and consumer information, but the idea came to nothing. We spent another year contacting forty women's organisations and clubs to see whether a combined newsletter giving reports of their work would serve a useful purpose as a liaison between organisations. The idea was that each would have a representative on an editorial board, the costs to be shared between the various organisations. The newsletter would act as a clearing-house for information between women's organisations and women generally. The response to our circular was poor so it was decided to disband the editorial board.

Mention must be made here of Eileen (Jim) Petrie who acted as chairwoman in the early years and so generously gave her time and professional skills while working full time in partnership with her husband and rearing seven children. Jim was a true example of 'find a busy person when you want a job well-done'. Her work for the Association was not confined to the editorial board. She was full of ideas to publicise the Association and raised a considerable amount of money on an exhibition of goods at the reception we gave for the IAW congress in 1961. Jim also sent a questionnaire to housewives asking for their ideas for the 'ideal home'. She put these together and the'Ideal Home' was constructed and exhibited at the Ideal Homes Exhibition. Jim helped with setting up our stalls at the RDS, designed and made our logo and has always been in the background with help and advice when we needed her. Jim helped with the organisation of our Silver Jubilee celebrations and has again come to our aid for our Golden Jubilee, in spite of illness.

Lillian Soiron also worked on the magazine for many years and was chairman of the editorial board during the difficult closing-down period and for the publication of the Silver Jubilee brochure.

In 1972 a new editorial board was set up by the initiative of Nora Browne, under her chairmanship. The new magazine, *Housewives Voice*, was produced three times yearly, the arrangement being that the printer collected the advertisements and kept the revenue from them, providing the IHA with an agreed number of copies which the IHA distributed free to our members and the public. Besides providing consumer information and giving news about our work, it was used for publicity at meetings and recruiting drives, and provided a valuable shop window for the Association. Many members of the original editorial board joined and helped with the new magazine.

In 1973 Nora Browne attended a meeting in Brussels to exchange ideas with other women's organisations in the EEC which produced magazines. It was decided that participating organisations would exchange magazines and provide a liaison among women in Europe. *Housewives Choice* ceased publication in 1980. Once again the soaring costs of production and the difficulties of competing for advertising against the daily press, radio and television had proved too much.

The editorial board continued to meet as it had taken over the publicity work for the IHA. It explored the possibility of putting a regular 'Housewives' programme on local community radio but this came to nothing, although we did take part in discussions by invitation from community stations. The board has arranged for IHA members to take part in various programmes on radio and television and has missed no opportunity to publicise our work.

Other committees have been set up, as needed, to deal with specific issues such as: the investigating sub-committee, set up in 1951 to carry out investigations in egg production and distribution - shop closing hours, price surveys of over forty different commodities, prices of imported china and crockery, prams, fish supplies. This committee gathered the data for the IHA submissions of evidence to the Prices Advisory Body and supplied price lists for *The Irish Housewife* which were also available to the public. Kathleen McLarnon Wells, then joint honorary secretary of the IHA, and later, Diana McClatchey, acted as secretaries of this hard-working committee which functioned for several years.

At various times constitution committees were set up, the original in 1948 to write our first constitution, when Mrs Hollinshead did valauble work in writing a draft. The constitution has been revised three times with the help of these committees.

A committee on education was set up in 1951 with Edith Cellem as secretary to prepare a memorandum on the Function and and Curriculum of Primary Schools which was submitted to the Council of Education.

In 1970 the IHA decided it was time to look at our image as we were not attracting younger women to the Association, so an ideas panel was set up and run by our younger members - Pat Davys, Mairéad Allen, Jean Hollinshead, Peggy O'Neill, Sheila Leech, Phil Moore, - to examine our structures and see how they could be brought up to date.

The ideas panel examined and advised on how to make more attractive the items sold at our sales of work and helped with the organisation of social events. They organised a series of coffee mornings in members' homes in different areas. They sent a questionnaire to members to find out their interests and skills and from the answers drew up an 'experts panel' of people who would undertake to keep themselves informed on specific subjects so that speakers could be provided to speak at meetings, or broadcast on radio or television, when required. Subjects listed for specialised study included: the law affecting women and children; home helps and nurses; the Constitution of Ireland; marketing practices; social benefits; the single parent and the law; votes at eighteen; school leaving age; pornography; the human environment; pollution.

The ideas panel functioned for five years and did a great deal to encourage new members to join and all members to play a more active part in the Association.

One result of the work of the ideas panel was a livelier interest in the environment and a working party was set up in 1975 to study the recycling of waste. As mentioned elsewhere the IHA has always been concerned about waste, refuse and its disposal, the litter in our towns and countryside. Now we were to study this subject in depth under the enthusiastic direction of Pat Davys. Other organisations working on the environment such as An Taisce and Friends of the Earth were contacted. A concentrated effort on the disposal of glass was made and the IHA alerted housewives to the existing recycling schemes and asked supermarkets to set up bottle banks.

An *ad hoc* committee for war on prices was formed in 1971 under the leadership of Mairéad Allen. The object of the *ad hoc* committee was to spearhead a protest against rising food prices, by making housewives aware of price changes. It contacted other women's organisations to join in consumer resistance to rising prices and members spoke on radio and television. This work was carried on the next year by a cost of living panel chaired by Betty Morrissey.

In the field of research the following members have made outstanding contributions to the IHA : Moira Guiney represented us on government and other bodies and acted as delegate to meetings and conferences, in addition to her work on the central committee and the various executive offices she held. Moira took meticulous notes at every meeting and produced concise informative reports which have been invaluable. She was always ready to take on research on any subject and draft memoranda. She spent herself in the service of the Association and worked until her final illness in 1991.

Marcella Hennessy was a long-standing member with a particular interest in the international committee and the editorial board. She also served on the central committee and as joint honorary secretary. Marcella was always ready to help with research, give evidence at enquiries or represent the IHA as a guest speaker at other organisations. She worked with us and for us until her death in 1990.

Mairéad Allen, who was appointed to the National Prices Commission to represent consumer interests from the IHA, did an enormous amount of research into prices, gave evidence at enquiries and spoke on radio and television as recorded elsewhere.

Gretta Morrisson has acted in several capacities on the central committee and most other committees and has made a contribution by researching subjects for memoranda. She has not spared herself in working for the IHA and has been engaged in research for this book.

Campaigns

Cleaner and cheaper milk

During investigations into the workings of the Dublin District Milk Board in 1942 we discovered that about sixty per cent of the milk sold in Dublin was pasteurised, three per cent was TT (tuberculin tested), leaving over thirty-five per cent loose milk, which could be germ-infected, particularly that which had travelled up from the country, much of it from a distance of over forty miles. A great deal of this milk was collected in the country by large wholesalers, 'flash' pasteurised, and transported to Dublin where it was sold loose. Producers were paid ninepence halfpenny per gallon and it was sold to the consumer at one shilling and eight pence loose, or two shillings and four pence bottled, per gallon.

The IHA wrote to the press, urging the Dublin District Milk Board to take over the distribution of milk in the Dublin district, 'thus cutting down expenses in transport and pasteurisation, and ensuring that all milk coming in will be clean milk'. Copies of our letter were sent to TDs (questions were asked in the Dáil), and to several doctors, including well-known paediatricians, some of whom supported our campaign and gave us information. Mrs E Stephens, former secretary of the Clean Milk Society (which functioned from 1926 until the Milk and Dairies Act was passed in 1935), spoke to the IHA on the aims of her society and urged us to see that existing legislation was enforced and stated that a drive for more TT milk was preferable to a campaign for pasteurisation of non-TT milk.

In July 1942 a deputation from the IHA was received by Dr Russell, MOH, Mr Dolan, Chief Veterinary Inspector, and Dr O'Sullivan of Dublin Corporation. We requested Dr Russell to apply to the Minister for Local Government and Public Health for the pasteurisation of all non-TT milk in the Dublin district. Dr Russell agreed in principle but stressed the difficulty of obtaining machinery during the 'emergency' and the possibility of a milk shortage due to transport difficulties. (During that period there was a seasonal shortage of milk during the winter before modern dairying methods were applied.)

Mr Dolan thought County Dublin farmers would be more willing to have their herds tuberculin tested rather than have pasteurisation introduced and advised us to contact the Dublin Cowkeepers Association. We decided to aim for a yearly increase in the numbers of TT herds and until 100 per cent TT was reached, all other milk should be pasteurised.

So the campaign continued. We enquired into the implementation of the 1935 Milk and Dairies Act. We investigated diseases, particularly those affecting children, caused by milk from cows suffering from bovine TB. We investigated the creameries and gathered information on the co-operatives. We met members of the Milk Board and visited several Dublin dairies. Letters were sent to the city hospitals and schools, asking which kind of milk they used, and to the School Meals Committee of Dublin Corporation asking how contracts for milk for schools were made.

We continued to gather information from 1942 to 1945, writing to the Minister, the Corporation and the press, campaigning for safe clean milk. On one occasion the Minister replied that 'before considering our letter he would be glad to know who are the members of your committee and how it is constituted' !

On 1 March 1945 the Minister for Local Government and Public Health announced the appointment of a Tribunal of Inquiry into the Supply of Milk to the Dublin Sale District, the terms of reference being to examine the supply of milk to distributors and consumers.

The IHA decided to give evidence to the tribunal and Andrée Skeffington, who was expecting a baby, undertook the huge task of collating the mass of data that we had collected on milk, and wrote the memorandum.

Unfortunately Andrée Skeffington was not well enough to attend the tribunal, so I gave the evidence. (I was completely surprised when the first question I was asked in cross-examination was, 'Where were you born ?' A witch hunt for foreign subversives? When I replied, 'Clones, County Monaghan' there was no comment and business proceeded.)

Our evidence dealt with the milk shortage in 1943, and the quality of milk brought from creameries to make up the deficiency; the difficulty of obtaining highest grade (TT), milk in some areas; the quality of milk; the defects of the Milk and Dairies Act (1935) in its application and interpretation; insufficient numbers of inspectors; the dual control of state and local authorities. We pointed out that only better-off people can afford adequate quantities of milk. Loose or pasteurised milk which does not stay fresh is uneconomic. We stressed the need for a revision of the Milk and Dairies act; an adequate number of inspectors; cleanliness of dairy shops and utensils; the building up of TT herds with gradual elimination of 'ordinary designation' milk and replacement by highest grade milk; a ban on export of first class cattle until our herds are scientifically rebuilt; better co-operation between the Departments of Public Health and Agriculture; a Joint Milk Board with consumer representation; municipalisation of Dublin's milk supply (If pure wholesome milk cannot be supplied as a commercial enterprise it should be done as a public service); Failing municipalisation, a subsidised scheme of cheap milk for all children under sixteen and all nursing and expectant mothers.

All the commercial interests in the production, distribution and marketing of milk were represented at the tribunal, as well as the Departments of Public Health and Agriculture. The Dublin District Milk Board gave evidence. Doctors gave evidence on behalf of the Public Health Department and the Medical Association, also veterinary surgeons and inspectors.

The public sittings of the tribunal lasted until the end of May. Either Edith Cellem or I attended each public session, backed up by a rota of note-takers and members anxious to show the consumer interest in this important inquiry, and so the IHA was well represented. We were disappointed that the general public did not show more interest. Only two individual witnesses to appear before the tribunal were listed as consumers. After presenting evidence each witness could be cross-examined. We used this opportunity to put some of our points across as questions.

The Report of the tribunal was published in December 1946. The tribunal, recognising the need for closer co-operation between the Departments of Agriculture and Public Health in controlling the supply of milk, advised that a new Milk Board be set up with a chair appointed by the government and two members nominated by the two Departments. It recommended a consultative committee to advise the Board on the representation of consumers, producers, retailers, distributors and members with specialised scientific knowledge. Unfortunately this committee was never set up.

The tribunal proposed that milk production should be organised in the prescribed area, to eliminate the risks of contamination and the increased costs of transporting milk by road and rail over long distances. The aim should be to produce more milk more efficiently, to raise the consumption of milk in the Dublin area to one pint per person per day. The tribunal stressed the need for: the improvement of dairy stock by cow-testing and elimination of uneconomic cows; efficient feeding of milch cows, particularly in winter; the control of cattle diseases.

The report recommended more research into the incidence and treatment of contagious abortion and mastitis which causes grave loss of milk production. But most important of all, it called for the planned eradication of bovine TB within a defined period, *not greater than 10 years*. This is one area in which the government has failed. The eradiction of bovine TB has never been given the priority and funding necessary to provide adequate control.

As a result of the findings of the tribunal all milk sold is pasteurised with the exception of highest grade milk and all milk is now produced under more hygienic conditions. In recent years the IHA has been greatly concerned with the modern additives to cattle feeding, such as hormones, and the possible effects on our milk and meat. We are still stressing the need for more inspectors to visit the various stages of production and more encouragement for farmers to seek early veterinary help in case of suspected disease.

Salvage of waste.

In 1942 the IHA was appalled at the waste of material which was so scarce in the 'Emergency' period. We wrote to Dublin Corporation suggesting that rubber, glass, tins and bones, as well as paper, should be salvaged, but the Corporation refused, saying that it had initiated a collection of waste paper which had failed from lack of co-operation by the public.

We discussed the whole question of salvage with Mr Erskine Childers, TD, then secretary to the Federation of Irish Manufacturers (later President of Ireland), who said that his organisation was anxious to have a central salvage scheme and suggested that we should approach the Department of Supplies. The Department of Industry and Commerce told us that a company had been formed to salvage waste paper. If successful, collection might be extended to other items.

The IHA then contacted Messrs O'Keefe (for animal by-products), the Dunlop Company and the Irish Glass Bottle Company, all of whom said they would be willing to collect salvage from dumps. We sent the Advisory Conference of Parish Councils a report of our work, suggesting that parish councils should organise house-to-house collections. The Conference was interested, but hesitant to act. It was strange that when raw materials were so scarce, collection of waste could not be organised, particularly as at times we imported waste paper.

Waste collections have been started spasmodically, mostly of paper and glass. These never lasted for long, because collections were not regular and housewives got fed up with piles of paper and broken glass lying around.

It was only when the dangers to the environment from tree-felling and the destruction of the rain forests were recognised that action was taken. Again the IHA lead a campaign for waste paper collection, re-cycling generally, and the setting-up of 'bottle banks' in 1975 when we had a special committee to dealt with salvage.

Litter

Over the years the IHA has written innumerable letters to the press appealing to the public not to dump litter in the countryside and on the streets of cities and towns, spoiling our image and jeopardising our tourist trade.

Once we were so desperate about the litter in Dublin it was suggested that members should dress in their best, take a broom and sweep the Dublin streets during Horse Show week in an effort to focus attention on litter. This was vetoed by some who thought it would not be 'nice'!

We have approached the local councils for more litter bins at bus stops and outside shops, more frequent refuse collections, more frequent sweeping of streets, but the usual reply is lack of funds to carry out these essential tasks. We welcomed the imposition of an 'on the spot' fine, but this is seldom, if ever, enforced. In spite of our best efforts, and those of many others, litter is still with us. The IHA is currently bracing itself for another litter campaign.

Lower Prices Council

In 1946 the Dublin Trades Union Council called a meeting, in the Mansion House, under the chairmanship of Mr E J Tucker of the TUC, to which trade unions, social and civil organisations and all political parties were invited to send representatives. The IHA attended the meeting and spoke on the need to control prices. It was decided to set up the Lower Prices Council with the aim to 'press unremittingly for fair prices for producer and consumer'. This had been one of the objectives of the IHA stated first in the 'Housewives Petition'. The constituent members of the Lower Prices Council were : The Irish Housewives Association; The Irish Conference of Professional and Service Associations; Irish Labour Party Clann na Poblacht; Dublin Trades Union Council; Women's Social and Progressive League; The Joint committee of Women's Societies and Social Workers.

The Lower Prices Council met in the offices of the TUC in Lower Gardiner Street with Mr Tucker as Chairman and Mrs Maureen O'Carroll of the Labour Party as honorary secretary. Members were divided into three sub-committees to investigate the costs of food, clothing and housing and to deal with complaints from consumers. I was appointed to represent the IHA and was elected honorary secretary of the executive co-ordinating committee of the Lower Prices Council in recognition of the work the IHA had done for price control.

The Lower Prices Council, with two political parties represented in its membership, had to be very careful to steer a neutral course. Mr Seán Lemass, when Minister for Industry and Commerce, said the LPC were 'meek as mice' when the coalition government sanctioned price increases, while Mr Morrissey, the Inter-Party Minister, complained the LPC were like 'yapping dogs at his heels' when in office and accused us of being 'mute inglorious Miltons' when Fianna Fáil was in power ! Perhaps we succeeded in striking a balance ?

During its first year the Lower Prices Council formed local branches in Dundalk, Drogheda and Waterford as well as in several Dublin districts. It sent out a questionnaire on prices to all interested persons, such as consumers and organisations from which much useful information was gathered. It held an open air meeting in O'Connell Street, when the public was told of the work of the LPC and asked to support it by refusing to pay high prices for essential goods.

Resulting from the investigations the LPC concentrated on the price of fruit and vegetables, which had long been a concern of the IHA, because the difference between the price paid to the producer and that paid by the consumer was too great, and varied considerably, from fifty per cent to 250 per cent in some cases. (A Dublin housewife had bought a cabbage inside which was a note saying 'I got two pence for this cabbage. What did you pay for it?' The answer was ten pence).

The IHA had always favoured a fair price for both producer and consumer, so we welcomed the findings of the LPC which confirmed our own conclusions that producer-consumer markets were necessary to cut out the unfair profits of the middlemen. Such markets would increase supplies of fresh vegetables and fruit by providing a convenient outlet for the small producer.

A deputation from the LPC was received at a meeting of Dublin Corporation where the need for producer-consumer markets was stressed. The LPC maintained that the existence of such markets would bring down prices generally. The Corporation promised to consider this proposal.

Meanwhile the IHA continued its investigations. Members went regularly to the Dublin Corporation market where fruit and vegetables were auctioned. They jotted down the prices paid by retailers and later in the day compared them with the prices asked in the shops. The IHA was also in touch with producers who were dissatisfied with the profits on their produce. The cost of production had also risen. We were told that cauliflower seed which cost nineteen shillings and six pence in 1939 cost four pounds in 1947.

The IHA wrote to the Minister asking that minimum prices to producers should be fixed concurrently with maximum retail prices. Each autumn we had watched the price of potatoes rise; the potato was a particularly important food during the 'emergency' when there was a severe shortage of bread and flour. In January 1947 the Minister introduced a graduated controlled price for potatoes at one shilling and eight pence per stone in January increasing by one penny per stone each month until it reached two shillings in June. We welcomed this scheme and asked for it to be extended to all root vegetables. During this period a farmer offered to sell the IHA potatoes at seven pounds per ton, a tempting offer which we had to refuse due to difficulties of storage and distribution.

The IHA welcomed the opportunity of working with the LPC, but continued with its own investigations and representations to the government, sharing information with the LPC. In the autumn of 1947 the LPC decided that an association of women's organisations could be an effective ally to combat the continuous rise in the cost of living and to work for a betterment of social conditions. To highlight women's right to participate in the national housekeeping a 'Women's Parliament' was set up to deal with the cost of living, and women from all over the state competed to act as Ministers. An enthusiastic first sitting, attended by delegates from most women's societies, was held at the Catholic Commercial Club on 7 October 1947 at which nine resolutions were passed. Members of the IHA proposed and spoke to resolutions criticising 'The Industrial Efficiency and Prices Bill 1947'; and demanded the setting up of municipal restaurants to serve simple meals at reasonable prices. They also demanded the provision of hot school meals to all school children. It was decided to form the Women's National Council of Action to deal with the resolutions passed on the cost of living. A committee was formed which included five members of the IHA. This council lasted for some years.

The Lower Prices Council concentrated on the setting up of a producer/consumer market, continuously lobbying Dublin Corporation. In 1948 the Corporation, after long deliberations, decided that such a market could be run in the existing Iveagh Market. Advertisements were put in the press asking producers to supply the market, and the reponse was encouraging. It was decided that the Agricultural Association of Ireland would run the market.

On 5 January 1949 the producer/consumer market was opened by the Lord Mayor at the Iveagh Market, Francis Street. The Corporation rented the premises (at £450/£500 per annum) to the Irish Agricultural Trading Company, a non-profit-making company set up for the express purpose of running the market. The running expenses of the market, staff, etc, came to 100 pounds per week and produce was sold at roughly ten per cent more than the wholesale market prices. Luxury fruit and vegetables and flowers were sold at a slightly higher profit in an effort to keep down the price of essentials. The establishment of the producer/consumer market provoked an outburst of protest from various vested interests: the wholesale market, retailers and the Retail Grocers, Dairies and Allied Trades Association (RGDATA), and the traders in Francis Street. By the end of 1949 the Agricultural Association of Ireland decided it would no longer run the market.

After much debate the Dublin Producer/Consumer Public Utility Society was formed to run the market with representation from Dublin Corporation, the Dublin Agricultural committee, the Dublin Wholesale market and the Lower Prices Council, representing the consumer. I was appointed to the management committee of the producer/consumer market and later served as chairman.

The producer/consumer market was well established by 1950. Housewives came by bus or car from all over Dublin to avail of the lower prices. The producer/consumer market owned a van and delivered once a week to several of the outlying districts on a cash basis. The suppliers were paid a guaranteed fixed price for goods which were sold at a ten per cent margin of profit to cover expenses. Much credit is due to the manager of the market, Mr Daniel O'Neill, for his expertise and his enthusiasm for the objectives of the market. He worked long hours, mostly with only one helper.

The producer/consumer market had a steadying effect on the prices of fruit and vegetables generally, and on one occasion brought down the price of potatoes quite spectacularly. When in a time of shortage prices had risen sharply, the producer/consumer market was able to sell a crop of potatoes bought earlier, at our normal margin of ten per cent. The producer/consumer market could usually sell potatoes below the maximum controlled price.

On 10 February 1954 we wrote to the city manager requesting an interview to discuss the position of the producer/consumer market as there had been a considerable drop in turnover during the previous six months. Bus fares had risen and this affected the numbers of housewives travelling from outside the area. At the same time there were fewer people living in the area due to the clearance of tenements and more competition from street hawkers in the area. The market also had difficulties with suppliers, as many of the producers preferred to gamble on prices in the wholesale market rather than accept a fixed price from the producer/consumer market, so that it was becoming more and more dependent on the wholesale market for produce. All this, combined with the reluctance of some of our customers to pay cash for deliveries, created serious difficulties for the market which had to work on such a low margin of profit and always paid cash to its suppliers. The producer/consumer market struggled on for another year under increasing difficulties and finally ceased trading in April 1955, although the Producer/Consumer Market Public Utility Society remained in existence for some time in the hope that it would be possible to start producer/consumer markets in more suitable areas. This did not happen in spite of the belief of the IHA and the LPC that such markets were a means of ensuring fair prices for producer and consumer.

Prices Advisory Body (PAB)

In January 1951 the Minister for Industry and Commerce set up the Prices Advisory Body, a tribunal of arbitration between manufacturers, retailers and consumers under the chairmanship of Justice Lavery. Miss McDowell, of the Women Workers Union was also a member of the tribunal. The IHA, which had been demanding the setting up of such a body, before which prices increases would have to be justified, welcomed the Prices Advisory Body and the Price Freeze Order, but expressed disappointment that no direct consumer representative sat on the PAB. However, we decided to make full use of this tribunal, submitting written evidence in advance and using the public hearings to question the grounds for proposed price increases and to suggest where existing prices needed investigation. This we consistently did during the term of the PAB, but we were disappointed that consumers generally did not make use of the tribunal to combat increases in prices, except for the Lower Prices Council, which, like ourselves, attended the public sessions, giving evidence and cross-examining manufacturers and traders seeking increases.

In 1951 public hearings of applications for increases in the the prices of jam, coal, meat, soap, laundry charges, gas and coke were held. In each case we sent in a memorandum, which entailed thorough research into costs of production. For example, in the case of meat, the cost of the cow at the market was traced, to the abattoir, to the cutting up of the carcass into edible meat and the disposal of all waste. All our investigations traced the product to its source, including costs such as wages, raw materials, transport, insurance. Having sent in our memorandum, members attended the hearing, gave further oral evidence and cross-examined the applicants. The preparation of these memoranda put a severe strain on our resources. It was sometimes most difficult to obtain the necessary information, but persistence sometimes brought reward. If we could not prevent an increase being granted, often at our insistence the increase was reduced. When the coal-merchants wanted to increase the price of coal to ten pounds, thirteen shillings per ton, only nine pounds, fifteen shillings was allowed, and later it was reduced to eight pounds, fifteen shillings.

Not only did we oppose the applications for price increases but the IHA applied to the PAB for a reduction in the price of babies' prams, starting a direct attack on price-rings. We won this battle and obtained a reduction in prices.

The IHA gave evidence at the inquiries of the Prices Advisory Body on bread, fish, eggs, tea, bacon, pork and pork products, turf, electricity, cocoa, sugar, bread and flour. The tribunal came to rely on the IHA to provide opposition to the demands of the manufacturers and retailers for price increases.

In 1958 the Prices Bill was passed, rescinding all existing controls and putting the onus on the consumer to prove that prices were too high. Prices Advisory committees were to be set up and the IHA pressed for the inclusion of consumer organisations on all such bodies. We also pointed out to the public that the best answer to unfair prices is consumer resistance.

Edith Cellem who was one of our chief researchers for the PAB after Andrée Skeffington had left us, was duly appointed to represent the IHA on a Prices Advisory Panel in 1958, but was never called. The Prices Advisory Panel was not called until 1964 when Doreen Johnston represented us. The panel investigated the manufacture and marketing of soap and detergents and also the manufacture and marketing of jams and marmalades and canned and processed foods. In 1965 the cost of housing at Blackbanks, Raheny was investigated. In 1966 further investigations were carried out into the price and marketing of meat and potatoes. In both cases they were found not to be unduly high. The IHA once more appealed to the public for consumer resistance.

Mrs Johnston was invited by the Minister for Industry and Commerce to be a member of the Prices Consultative committee, set up to advise on commodities and services requiring investigation. In 1968 Mrs Johnston was again invited to join the Government Prices Advisory Body, which was comprised of twelve independent members, any one of whom may be called by the Minister to form a committee to examine commodities or services in need of investigation. This Body was not called,

105

although the Minister on several occasions published lists of approved prices.

In 1973 the Minister for Industry and Commerce set up the National Consumer Advisory committee to advise on legislation to protect consumer interests and promote consumer education. Moira Guiney and Betty Morrissey were our represenatives and did useful work. In the previous year, 1972, the National Prices Commission, (NPC), was set up to operate a measure of price control through restraints at manufacturing and wholesale levels and to allow competition to keep prices down. The National Prices Commission met once a week from 1972 until 17 January 1986 when it was disbanded. Thorough investigation of all factors influencing the cost of goods and services were carried out. Approved prices were published monthly and a statutory price control was in place, which over fourteen years kept down the cost of living in Ireland.

Mairéad Allen was appointed to represent the IHA as consumers on the NPC and attended every Tuesday morning for fourteen years, being paid a small remuneration, half of which she generously donated to the IHA. (One of our sources of income in the IHA was the donation of half of any fees earned from television or radio broadcasts.) Mairéad had a flair for this type of work and a good head for figures, and endless patience in research. The IHA was fortunate to have such a dedicated representative, who besides making a valuable contribution to the NPC gave excellent reports of her work to the IHA.

In his press release covering the disbandment of the Commission, the Minister for Trade, Commerce and Tourism, Mr John Bruton, announced 'major new measures to promote competition in the economy'. To date we have seen no implementation of these measures and as a consumer organisation we deplore that there is no control, surveillance or monitoring by a body on which the consumer is directly represented.

Consumer Protection

From the late fifties Ireland was much concerned with the debate about our entry into the EEC. As the only voluntary organisation then working for consumer protection the IHA received funding from the government to enable them to send delegates to meetings abroad. The chairwoman, Maureen Curran, attended a conference on consumer protection called by the European Productivity Agency of the Organisation for European Economic Co-operation (OEEC), held in Paris in October, 1957. Mrs Curran reported that Ireland was behind most other European countries in consumer protection. As a result of this and the many complaints we had received concerning Irish manufactured goods we approached the Federation of Irish Industries with suggestions which we hoped would lead to greater confidence in Irish goods.

In April 1960, as chairwoman, I attended an OEEC meeting in Paris on consumer information. This was attended by delegates from twelve European countries and the USA and an observer from Israel, as well as from bodies such as the International Standards Organisation, the newly-formed International Office of Consumers' Unions (IOCU).

The purpose of the meeting was: to exchange experience on the activities of organisations concerned with comparative testing of consumer goods, quality certification and informative labelling of goods; also to investigate possibilities of closer co-operation between such organisations in view of the widening of European markets.The IHA was delighted to contact consumer organisations abroad because, from our foundation, we had worked on consumer protection in isolation.

The IHA asked that the following points should be discussed: the initial steps in setting up a bureau for the testing of consumer goods and the qualifications of the staff required; the financing of such bureaux; government aid, grants from manufacturers of products; which countries have legislation

107

requiring the informative labelling of goods for home and export markets; the cost of informative labelling and packaging of goods to the consumer.

The final conclusions of the meeting were: the cost of comparative testing was a deterrent in all countries; all existing facilities for testing such as state and university laboratories, standard institutes and public analysts, should be utilised; government grants should be sought provided the consumers' organisations remained independent; funds can be raised by sale of information bulletins to the public to supplement income from members' subscriptions; the legal aspects of comparative testing should not deter consumer testing of goods; consumers must be responsible for information published; producers are reluctant to face adverse publicity by defending inferior goods.

In 1961 I attended an international women's meeting organised by the Women's Committee of the French Organisation of the European Movement, held in Paris. Representatives from fourteen European countries attended. Lectures and discussions on the following subjects took place: The Position in Europe in 1961; Europe in a World Context; Women and International Education; Women and the Common Market; Consumer Protection; Women and European Institutions.

It was evident that women believed that the bonds between their countries should not be merely commercial and economic, but cultural and educational also. At a similar meeting in Paris in 1960 the Comité d'Action Feminine Europeanne (CAFE), had been formed. This was the first effort to establish a liaison between women representatives of European movements and women's organisations working to build a United Europe and promote a better understanding between European people.

In 1962 our work for consumer protection intensified. Miss Eirlys Roberts, editor of *Which*, the organ of the British consumers, had spoken at our previous AGM stressing the desirability of a well-informed public who would recognise the quality and suitability of the goods on offer and the need for comparative testing of goods to ensure this. We approached the government and the Federation of Irish Industries on the need for informative labelling, which was compulsory in many countries to which Ireland exported goods and had to comply with these regulations.

In March 1962 our vice-chairwoman, Eileen Hackett, attended a conference of the IOCU in Brussels from which she brought back much useful information to enforce our campaign for a well-informed and vocal body of consumers, who would not only protect their own interests but also encourage a high standard for Irish goods.

We continued our campaign, asking consumers to demand a high quality of goods and services and to make complaints to the relevant people when standards were not met. We were concerned not only with quality, price and distribution, but with the handling of goods, demanding a high standard of hygiene in foodshops. We submitted memoranda to the Minister for Industry and Commerce and delegations were received on more than one occasion. We used the media whenever we could to educate the public regarding their rights as consumers. Meanwhile we kept in touch with the IOCU and the Consumers' Association of the UK and the Consumers' Union of Japan in particular, so we had a good idea of happenings abroad.

In June 1964 our joint honorary secretary, Doreen Johnston, attended the conference of IOCU in Oslo at which twenty-two nations were represented and papers were read on consumer education, informative labelling, standards for comparative testing, joint international testing. The need for consumer education was stressed, especially radio and television talks which would reach the public, on availability, price, quality and service.

The IHA set up an *ad hoc* committee to deal with consumers' complaints to be used by those who themselves failed to get satisfaction. We pressed for the price, weight, list of contents and country of origin to be clearly marked on all packaged goods, the type of material, washing and dry-cleaning instructions to be marked on all clothing and also safety instructions to be given with electrical and similar goods.

In June 1966 our chairwoman, Maude Rooney, accompanied by the honorary secretary, Doreen Johnston, represented the IHA at a conference of IOCU in Israel. After their return the whole question of consumer protection was discussed by the central committee of the IHA once again. Ireland was behind many other countries in the whole area of consumer protection and it was felt steps must be taken to rectify this. It was necessary to form a body of both men and women which could concentrate on this one area of the work of the IHA and to raise funds to carry out such work.

The IHA called a public meeting in the Shelbourne Hotel on 7 September 1966 to which all who were interested were invited to hear Mr Van Veen, secretary of IOCU, speak on the essential functions of a consumer organisation. A steering committee was set up who arranged a further public meeting in the Metropolitan Hall on 29 October 1966, at which a Council was elected to run the Consumers Association of Ireland (CAI): chairwoman, Maude Rooney, IHA; recording secretary, Marcella Hennessy, IHA; correspondence secretary : Norman Spendlove; joint treasurers : Peg Hyland, IHA, and Robert Rumball. The council members were Dillie O'Malley O'Donoghue, IHA, Kate Moynihan, Hilda Tweedy, IHA, Lillie O'Callaghan, IHA, Seán O'Sullivan, Captain Myles O'Malley O'Donoghue, Norman Smythe, Quentin Cribbon and Alan Porter, Director, Standards Division, Institute for Industrial Research and Standards.

The aims of the CAI are to help the consumer gain more knowledge of goods and services on offer, to promote a better service, proper packaging and handling of goods, a standard for advertising and labelling, better value for money and better services, including hire of goods and hire-purchase facilities. The Institute for Industrial Research and Standards and the National Buy Irish Council both promised their support to the CAI.

The IHA was very pleased with the setting-up of the CAI. This left us with more time and resources to carry out the rest of our work. We continued to deal with specific complaints from our members and the public, to advise consumers in dealing with their own complaints and to seek a better standard of hygiene in dealing with food. The establishment of a strong CAI has greatly strengthened consumer protection in Ireland.

Epilogue

One of the objects of writing the story of the Irish Housewives Association is to make people aware of the link with the feminist movement in the past. So many people believe that the women's movement was born on some mystical date in 1970, like Aphrodite rising from the waves. It has been a long continuous battle in which many women have struggled to gain equality, each generation adding something to the achievements of the past.

It has been an interesting experience to sit back from present-day women's problems and research the work of the Irish Housewives Association, which as well as covering women's issues also deals with consumer interests. I have learnt about many aspects of our work of which I was not really aware before, which has strengthened my belief in the importance of research and assessment of work.

The link between those engaged in women's studies with the grass root women's organisations is vital and could be further strengthened to their mutual benefit. Organisations are so occupied with work in hand that there is no time, or funds, to review regularly the progress they are making. This is particularly true of the Irish Housewives Association. Like the proverbial housewife, our 'work is never done'. We can only deal with the issues as they appear daily. The present problems and the development of new trends is as important as the study of women's achievements in the past.

The whole structure of society, and with it the structure of women's organisations, has changed in the life span of the IHA. There is practically no domestic help, neither can the housewife rely on help from the extended family; the grannies and aunties are working outside the home now. Young women are either fully occupied with domestic duties or coping with the dual role of bread-winner and housewife. There is neither time nor money to spend on voluntary work.

This is not just an Irish problem. Women at international level are discussing ways and means of attracting young women into their organisations. Women's organisations have also changed. New groups are set up to deal with specific issues such as rape, single parenting, battered wives. Perhaps they are all the more effective for that reason; they can put all their energies into one cause. At the time the IHA was founded there was no other organisation dealing with consumerism and the status of women in the way we did. The Irish Countrywomen's Association, with which we have always had close and friendly relations, came nearest. Based on their nationwide guilds they have been able to make an enormous contribution to improving the lives of Irish women in both town and country.

For some years the IHA has failed to attract sufficient new young members to carry on. We have become an ageing group and have lost many of our active members who carried out research. With our loss of membership comes loss of revenue, making it impossible to continue the Association in its present form. Rather than fade away into oblivion the Association has decided to dissolve itself and make the occasion of our Golden Jubilee a celebration of our achievements over the last fifty years. We hand over our work with confidence to the Council for the Status of Women and the Consumers Association of Ireland, both of which came into being as a result of the initiative of the Irish Housewives Association.

The IHA is proud to trace its connection with the Irish Women Citizens Association, and through them to the Irish Women's Suffrage Society and the Women's League for Suffrage and Local Government, and to be the link between them and the Council for the Status of Women and the present women's movement. In this way we have played our part.

We hope that we have fulfilled our orginal aim, at least to some extent: 'To unite housewives, so that they may realise, and gain recognition for, their right to play an active part in all spheres of planning for the Community'. The IHA has certainly been active over fifty years. Women are now much more aware of their own potential, and recognition of this is increasing. Progress has been made. Our laws have been changed to promote equality, but attitudes to, and the implementation of, these reforms still need attention. Who would have thought in 1942 that women could move from the kitchen to Aras un Uachtaráin?

It is interesting to note that many of the problems affecting women today were first identified by women so long ago. Very little has been achieved overnight. It has been a long hard haul, each generation building on the work of those who have gone before. The Irish Housewives Association is proud and happy to have been a link in that chain.

Chairwomen of the IHA

1942-1992

Susan Manning 1942-1947

Susan Manning was one of the signatories of the Housewives Petition in 1941, and was one of those who suggested the formation of an Association. From girlhood Susan had been interested in the struggle for women's rights and was active in the Irish Women Citizens Association. She was always anxious to encourage younger women to play their part. Until her death in 1964 she maintained a lively interest in the IHA.

Marie Mortished 1947-1949

Marie Mortished joined soon after our foundation and served on the committee before her two years as chairwoman. She was deeply involved in our work and persuaded many of her friends to join the IHA. To our regret she left Ireland in 1949 to live in California where she died in 1964.

Jean Coote 1949-1953

Early in her married life, Jean Coote dedicated herself to work for political and economic freedom, equal opportunities and fair play for women. An active member of the Irish Women Citizens Association, she was instrumental in negotiating its incorporation into the IHA in 1948. In 1950 Jean Coote stood as an

114

Independent candidate for election to Dublin Corporation, but was narrowly defeated. In spite of illness she carried out her duties as chairwoman with vision and wisdom.

Beatrice Dixon 1954-1955

Beatrice Dixon is well-known for her interest in women's civil and political rights. As chairwoman she represented the IHA at the international committee of IAW in London. In 1957 she stood as an Independent candidate for Dáil Eireann, sponsored by the IHA and remained in the running until the seventh count. Beatrice was one of the first women to serve on a jury in Ireland. Although no longer active in the Association she has remained a member.

Elsie Sawier 1955-1956

Elsie Sawier joined the IHA in the forties and served on the central committee for several years where she was noted for the high standard of her work as minutes secretary. Mrs Sawier represented the IHA on deputations to the Minister for Agriculture and to government departments and on the Freedom from Hunger Campaign. She served on the social and international committees and worked on the editorial board, contributing regularly to *The Irish Housewife*.

Maureen Curran 1956-1959

Maureen Curran joined the IHA in 1953 and served in many different roles, including chairwoman, vice-chairwoman and honorary treasurer. As chairwoman she was received by the late President of Ireland, Mr Seán T O'Kelly, to introduce Miss Ester Graff from Denmark, then president of IAW. In 1957 Maureen went to Paris on a government grant to represent the

IHA at an OECC Conference on Consumer Protection. She represented us on the Joint Committee of Women's Societies and was elected its chairwoman. She was excellent in this role due to her unusual gift of knowing every member by name. She was made an honorary member of the IHA in recognition of her outstanding services.

Hilda Tweedy 1959-1962

Hilda Tweedy, a founder member of the IHA, served as joint honorary secretary from 1942 to 1951. She represented the IHA on the Lower Prices Council and was a member of the management board of the producer/consumer market, 1949-1955. As chairwoman she represented the IHA in Paris at a OEEC meeting on consumer protection in 1960 and at the women's committee of the French European Movement in 1961. Hilda worked on the editorial board of *The Irish Housewife* for twenty years. She joined the international sub-committee when it was formed and through it, has represented IHA at IAW congresses from 1949 to 1986. Hilda Tweedy represented the IHA on the *Ad Hoc* Committee on the Status of Women, acting as chairwoman, and also was a founder member and first chairwoman of the Council for the Status of Women of which she is now an honorary member. In 1990 Trinity College, Dublin conferred on her the Honorary Degree of Doctor in Laws.

Eileen Hackett 1962-1965

Eileen Hackett joined the IHA in 1950, already interested in women's affairs through active membership of the Women's Social and Progressive Club. She served on the central committee as minutes secretary, joint honorary secretary, vice-chairwoman and chairwoman. As vice-chairwoman she was organiser for the IAW congress and it was largely due to her hard work and unfailing cheerfulness that the congress was such a happy event. As chairwoman she represented the IHA at the International Organisation of Consumers Unions Conference in Brussels in 1964, and in 1965 at the Memorial Service to Teresa Garnett, held in London. Eileen was chairwoman of the international sub-committee for several years and led deputations to IAW congresses on several occasions, notably in India in 1973. She is a founder member of the *Ad Hoc* committee and the Council for the Status of Women. No job in the IHA was too big or too little for Eileen to tackle.

Maude Rooney 1965-1968

Maude Rooney joined the IHA in 1949 and acted as honorary treasurer, minutes secretary and joint honorary secretary before becoming chairwoman. She was also an active member of the social and international sub-committees and the editorial board, and represented us on the women's advisory committee of the Institute for Industrial Research and Standards. In 1966 she attended the Fourth Biennial Conference of the International Organisation of Consumer Unions in Israel. Inspired by this experience she threw her energy into the formation of a comprehensive consumer organisation in Ireland which culminated in the foundation of the

Consumers Association of Ireland in 1966, to which Maude Rooney was elected as its first chairwoman. She gave her best to the Association until her death in 1975.

Nora F Browne 1968-1972 and 1985-1989

Nora Browne was born in Rathfarnham, County Dublin and educated at Wesley College and Trinity College, Dublin, where she obtained a BA degree in Arts and later an MA.

Nora has been a member of the IHA since the '50s but she has not confined her interest to any one women's organisation. She has been vice-president of the National Federation of the Business and Professional Women's Clubs and President and founder member of the Dublin Club, President of the Dublin International Soroptimist Club, President of DUWGA, Founder and President of the Wesley Old Girls Association, chairwoman of the Irish Housewives Association, Member of the First National Commission on the Status of Women, Member of the Irish Goods Council, these last two were government appointments. Nora Browne served two periods as chairwoman of the IHA and three periods as honorary treasurer, between 1975 and 1991.

Betty Morrissey 1972-73

Betty Morrissey is a founder member of the IHA and was our first honorary treasurer, who steered us through our financial teething troubles during her five years of office. She acted as treasurer of our election fund in 1957 when we put up three Independent women candidates and actually left us with money in hand for our next election campaign.

During her term as chairwoman three new branches of the IHA were formed, at Athlone,

118

Dundalk and Carlow. Betty has served on most of the sub-committees and the editorial board, of which she was honorary treasurer. She was appointed by the government to represent the IHA on The National Consumers Advisory Council in November 1973.

Molly Cranny 1973-75 and 1978-81

Molly Cranny who is a Dubliner, born and bred, joined the IHA in 1963 and immediately became immersed in our work. First she acted as minutes secretary to the central committee, then as joint honorary secretary from 1970-73. She was a member of the editorial board, the social committee and the international committee, and she represented the IHA at conferences in Paris, London and Brussels. In 1974 the IHA organised a protest march, led by Molly Cranny, through Dublin to protest against rising prices. Over 3,000 took part, passers-by joining us in the street, and a letter was handed in to the Minister of Industry and Commerce.

Maura O'Rourke 1975-1978

Maura O'Rourke was born in County Waterford and grew up in Youghal. After she left school she came to live in Dublin and worked in Eason & Co, the booksellers. Though aware of the IHA from its foundation, she joined in 1961 when her children were older. Maura quickly became involved and served as minutes secretary and vice-chairwoman, as well as working on committees, before being elected national chairwoman. As chairwoman, Maura visited all our branches and acted as hostess to the IAW board meeting held in Trinity Hall in 1977. Maura represented the IHA on the Consumer Education committee which reported to the government on matters pertaining to the proposed Consumer Protection Bill. She has always been most generous in lending her house for our social and fund-raising efforts.

Moira Guiney, 1981-1985

Moira Guiney began her career as a civil servant with the Revenue Commissioners. In the mid-60s, when her three sons were reared, she joined the IHA; from then she worked with dedication and great enthusiasm until her final illness in 1991. In addition to being chairwoman, she served as vice-chairwoman, and joint honorary secretary, and represented the IHA on various bodies such as the VAT Council, the National Standards Authority of Ireland, the National Consumers Advisory Council, the Federation of Urban and Rural Associations, the Consumers Standards Consultative committee, the National Fruit and Vegetable Federation (ACOT) and CAP.

Ciarin Doherty 1989-1992

Ciarin Doherty was born in Dalkey, Co Dublin and educated at Sion Hill, Blackrock. After school she worked at Shannon Airport. Ciarin has always been interested in the Irish language and speaks it where possible. She represented the Irish Federation of Women's Clubs on the Council for the Status of Women at its foundation. Ciarin represented the IHA on the Keep Sunday Special Committee and is on the Consumer Standards Consultative Committee. With her many interests Ciarin has been an excellent figurehead for the IHA, publicising our work and increasing our membership.

Milestones

1941 The Housewives' Petition is presented to the Government signed by fifty-one housewives. Over 600 signatures collected later that year.

1942 The Irish Housewives Association is formed; campaigns for fair distribution of essential commodities at a fair price for producer and consumer.

1943 The IHA investigates milk supply and start a campaign for safer, cleaner, cheaper milk; examines the marketing of fruit and vegetables; joins the Emergency Conference of Women's Societies; organises street march to focus needs of children especially in area of school meals.

1944 IHA secures price control for cooking fats. Survey of cleanliness of food shops makes headlines in the press.

1945 Three victories: potato prices reduced by ten pence per stone: price of oranges evidence presented to Department; government appoints Tribunal of Inquiry into Dublin milk supply and IHA presents evidence.

1946 Investigations into the fruit and vegetable racket. IHA supports ICA idea of producer/consumer markets. Campaigns for cleaner handling of food. Sends recommendations to Minister on proposed Public Health Bill. Publishes *The Irish Housewife*.

1947 The Lower Prices Council formed. IHA plays active role in it. Milk Tribunal Report is published, embodying IHA evidence and suggestions. First branch founded in Dun Laoghaire.

1948 Branches of IHA formed at New Ross, Mount Merrion, Skerries and Bray. Irish Women Citizens Association incorporated in the IHA. Affiliation with the International Alliance of Women.

Three memoranda presented to government: The High Cost of Living; Necessary Improvements in Public Health Services; Reasons for Emigration from Ireland.

1949 Dublin Producer/Consumer Market opens. IHA

represented on Advisory Board to Corporation Marketing Committee through the Lower Prices council. Four IHA members attend Fifteenth Triennial Congress of the IAW in Amsterdam. IHA studies school premises and County Council housing schemes. IHA presses for school meals. IHA represented on the 'Buy Irish' Committee.

1950 IHA opposes removal of price controls. Discussion with Department on prices of oranges, bacon and sausages. Memorandum on Food Hygiene sent to Minister. Investigations into handling of food, disposal of street refuse, conditions in slaughter houses. IHA chairman, Jean Coote, stands as Independent candidate for Dublin Corporation; narrowly defeated.

1951 Government sets up Prices Advisory Body, (PAB). IHA opposes price increases for jam, coal, meat, soap, laundry charges, gas and coke. Food Hygiene Regulations become law. IHA memorandum on Functioning and Curriculum of Primary Schools sent to Minister.

1952 PAB: IHA opposes price increases for milk, coal and groceries. Applies for reduction in cost of prams and wins case. IHA meet Parliamentary Secretary to Minister for Agriculture on Sea Fisheries Bill. Three IHA delegates attend IAW congress in Naples.

1953 PAB: IHA presents evidence on price of sea fish, eggs and gas. IHA deputations to government on Restrictive Trades Practices Bills and White Paper on 1952 Health Bill.

1954 PAB: IHA presents evidence on price of cocoa. Questionnaire sent to Dáil candidates on price control, child welfare, education and clean food legislation. IHA urges extension of free milk schemes. Restrictive Trades Practices regarding Chemists' goods are investigated. IAW: Two IHA delegates attend summer School in Denmark on Social Services.

1955 PAB: IHA opposes increase in prices of tea, bacon, pork, turf, coal and gas.

1956 PAB: IHA opposes increases in prices of electricity, bread and flour, oatmeal, jam, cocoa, laundry prices, sugar and glassware. IHA asks for inquiry into price and quality of meat. IHA opposes levy on oranges and protests against increase in bus fares. IHA gives evidence on sale of patent medicines and baby foods. IHA asks for precautions against spread of polio.

1957 IHA suggestions included in Report into Supply and Distribution of Grocery Provisions. IHA attends inquiry into supply of goods to co-operative wholesale societies. IHA urges Minister to act on recommendation of Commission on patent medicines and baby foods. IHA protests against decontrol of bread and flour prices and suggests supply of turf to OAPs during summer. Levy on oranges removed due to IHA. IHA sponsors three Independent women candidates for Dáil. Visit of IAW president, Ester Graff. IHA chairwoman attends Consumer Protection Conference held in Paris by the European Productivity Agency. IHA asks for representation on proposed Prices Advisory Committee.

1958 IHA investigates price, supply, variety, quality and freshness of fish. IHA protests against increases in cost of bread and children's lunch-time fares. IHA asks for control of supplies and prices of the 1958 potato crop. IHA writes to An Taoiseach asking for immediate steps to arrest the rise in the cost of living. IHA representative appointed to serve on Prices Advisory Committee. IHA meets Federation of Irish Manufacturers to discuss cut, size and quality of their clothing. IHA representative appointed to the Advisory Committee of the Institute of Industrial Research and Standards. IHA urges registration and inspection of Nursing Homes, cleaner handling of food and stresses need for anti-litter campaign. IHA asks Minister to provide adequate training for Women Police and Probation Officers. IHA delegate attends IAW congress in Athens.

1959 IHA holds symposium on fish and protests against price of bread and removal of standard weight of loaf. Price of turf briquettes is investigated and subsequently reduced. Public warned about deceptive packaging of dried fruit. IHA asks that suppliers of 'Synthetic cream' display notice to that effect. IHA asks for implementation of by-laws regarding litter, and more frequent bin collections. IHA again urges registration of nursing homes on suitability of premises and number of trained nurses. IHA protests against duty on imported medical drugs. IHA sends memorandum on juvenile delinquency to Minister and asks for women to serve on juries on the same terms as men.

1960 IHA asks that Prices Advisory Panels investigate before price increases are granted. IHA deputation to Department to discuss profits on school uniforms; action leads to drop in prices. IHA delegate attends Conference in Paris held by the European Productivity Agency of OEEC. Minister discusses IHA report of Conference. IHA asks for introduction of informative labelling of goods, provision of laboratory for testing goods and a bulletin for consumer information. IHA deputation to Department to discuss registration of nursing homes. IHA asks government to delay Fluoridation Bill until public are better informed.

1961 IHA asks Minister to reduce price of butter by saving in export subsidy. IHA protests against price rises and asks again for Prices Advisory Panel to be called. IHA warns consumers against incorrect labelling of 'bargain' goods during sales. IHA writes to Irish Pharmaceutical Society on standards for Irish drugs. IHA approaches the Federation of Irish Industries, on informative labelling and comparative testing of goods. IHA asks women to use votes, and when suitable, to vote for women in the general elections. We appeal again for women jurors on the same terms as men. IHA advises girls seeking jobs outside of Ireland to investigate conditions thoroughly. IHA requests Gardaí to enforce law prohibiting children from flag-selling on the streets. IHA delegate attends meeting of Women's Committee of the French European Movement in Paris to discusss women's part in the European Movement. The IHA hosts the IAW congress in Dublin, which is attended by 350 women from abroad.

1962 IHA campaigns for informative labelling on packaged goods and textiles. IHA delegate attends Conference of International Organisation of Consumer's Unions in Brussels. IHA asks for the cost of Health and Social Services to be borne by the Central Fund. IHA supports protest of Irish Nurses Association against use of title 'Nurse' by unqualified persons. IHA holds public meeting to discuss Fluoridation of Water. IHA memorandum sent to Minister suggesting change in laws affecting women and children - inheritance, guardianship, marriage age, age of adoption and jury service. After renewed protest against child collectors for charities Minister fixes minimum age of fourteen. Minister asked to prohibit importation and sale of air guns. Garda Síochána asked to act against sale of illegally imported fireworks.

1963 IHA celebrate twenty-first Anniversary. IHA deputation to Department discusses informative labelling and comparative testing of goods. Drogheda branch protests against rise in price of coal and protests against unjustified overcharging prior to introduction of turnover tax, and sent price increases to Minister, who appointed regional price investigators. IHA urges Commission on Court Procedure to introduce jury service for women on the same terms as men. IHA writes to Minister on the rises in hospital charges and urges registration of all nursing homes. IHA writes about treatment of children in institutions. IHA writes to Lord Mayor asking that no further bingo saloons be licensed in O'Connell Street; request is passed by Corporation.

1964 IHA encourages consumers to make on-the-spot complaints when not satisfied with goods or services. We urge the public to see that meat prices are displayed in butchers' shops as legally required. IHA delegate attends Conference of Consumers Unions in Oslo. IHA memorandum on the Adoption Bill presses for the age of adoption to be raised to twenty-one years. IHA asks that men found soliciting on the streets should be liable to prosecution on the same terms as women.

1965 We advise members to seek alternatives to higher priced cuts of meat. IHA delegate invited by Minister to become a member of the Prices Consultative Committee. Women's Advisory Committee to Institute for Industrial Research and Standards investigates the quality and durability of schoolbags, Irish-made shoes, pram harnesses, and aluminium holloware, the safety of toys and the flammability of children's clothing. IHA writes to Minster expressing dismay at leniency of sentences passed on offenders in cases of indecent assault on young girls, and protests against the sale of alcohol to teenagers. IHA asks for women to be represented on government delegations to International Labour Organisation.

1966 Chairwoman attends Conference of International

organisation of Consumer Unions in Israel. On 28 October the Consumers Association of Ireland formed. IHA writes to government on proposed legislation for pre-packed goods. IHA reports bad conditions of public conveniences and lack of amenities for women to Dublin Corporation, County Councils and Bord Fáilte. IHA writes to Dublin Health Authority on conditions in homes for the aged. IHA sends memorandum to Department on health services and gains representation on the Food Hygiene Advisory Committee. Formation of Limerick and Cavan branches of IHA. Branches in Drogheda, Cork, Limerick and Cavan survey meat prices. IHA represented on the Food Hygiene Advisory Committee by the Minister for Health.

1967 IHA continues work with Women's Advisory Committee of the Institute of Industrial Research and Standards. Requests the embargo on imported tomatoes should not be imposed until price of home grown tomatoes drops. Supports principle of remission of rates and free travel for old age pensioners. IHA delegation attends IAW congress in London; affiliates asked to examine the status of women in their country. Mrs Carmel Gleeson, sponsored by the IHA, elected as an Independent to the County Council.

1968 IHA with the BPW calls meeting to discuss status of women in Ireland. Ad Hoc Committee formed to examine need for National Commission on the Status of Women. IHA organise Symposium on Human Rights. IHA Cork branch weight of loaf and fancy bread and protests about poor quality coal at top prices. Limerick branch investigates price of school uniforms; Complains about quality of Limerick water supply. Dun Laoghaire branch of the IHA re-formed.

1969 Memoranda sent to government on control of air Pollution and on Merchandise Marks Bill. IHA demands that agriculture be supported by exchequer grants instead of consumer levies.

1970 The IHA, with help of branches, organises National food Hygiene Week under patronage of Minister for Health. Government sets up National Commission on the Status of Women. IHA delegation attends IAW Congress in Konigstein. IHA organises seminar on Education. IHA branch formed in

Wexford.

1971 *Housewives Voice* published. IHA, with the National Development Association, organise a 'Good Housekeeping Irish Style' fortnight as part of Buy Irish Campaign. Interim Report of National Commission on the Status of Women on Equal Pay published. IHA delegate appointed to National Prices Commission.

1972 IHA Chairwoman attends International Committee of IAW in Finland. IHA hosts visits of a member of Deutscher Frauenring to arrange exchanges and of young Japanese woman who came to Ireland to attend language school. IHA organises 'Women's Parliament'. Report of the National Commission on the Status of Women (Beere Report) published. Council for the Status of Women formed to implement the Beere Report. Branches of IHA formed at Naas, Carlow, Dundalk, and Athlone. IHA sends submission to EEC Committee on Economic Affairs and development on drawing up the 'European Consumer Protection Charter'.

1973 IHA representative on NPC attends EEC Round Table Conference on Consumer Affairs. IHA protests about advertisement for vacancy with pay discrimination on sex basis. IHA delegation attends IAW Congress in New Delhi. IHA forms new Branch in Ennis.

1974 IHA organises protest march against rising prices. Central Committee of IHA received at Aras An Uachtaráin. Members of Deutscher Frauenring from Kronberg visit IHA. IHA organise 'Good Housekeeping Exhibition and National Hygiene Week' in conjunction with NDA at Ireland House. Cork Branch protests against EEC proposal to spend over two million pounds advertising meat; meets the Minister to discuss meat for pensioners. Members of Branch took part in Dublin protest march. Dundalk Branch hosts four members of Deutscher Frauenring.

1975 UN International Women's Year. IHA member on Irish delegation to UN Conference in Mexico nominated by WRC. Two IHA delegates attend Les Journées Internationales de Paris and IAW Board meeting in Paris. IHA members support Dublin peace march; Ennis branch organises local peace march. Sixteen

IHA members visit Deuscher Frauenring in Kronberg.

1976 IHA delegation goes to IAW Congress in New York. Two members of Deutscher Frauenring interested in Peace Movement visit Ireland. IHA calls for support for home-produced fruit and vegetables and Irish goods generally.

1977 IHA hosts IAW board meeting held at Trinity Hall, Dublin. IHA holds press conference asking all political parties to examine reasons for low representation of women in the Dáil and Seanad. IHA writes to Government asking for women on Irish delegation to UN Disarmament Conference. Government sets up Employment Equality Agency. IHA delegate to NCP attends International Symposium on Consumer Affairs in Brussels.

1978 IHA becomes full member of COFACE. IHA organises Public Meeting on 'Women's Contribution to World Peace'. IHA member attends IAW Board meeting in Teheran.

1979 IHA chairman attends European Symposium on 'The Year of the Child and the European Community' organised by COFACE in London. 75th Anniversary of IAW. Two IHA delegates attend IAW Conference in Monrovia.

1980 IHA member attends UN Mid- Decade Conference in Copenhagen as observer on government delegation nominated by CSW. IHA arranges two public meetings with aid from EEC on 'Habitat' and 'Energy Options in the '80s'.

1981 IHA deputation received by Department to discuss supermarket legislation. IHA member attends IAW Board meeting in Cairo.

1982 IHA sent two delegates attend the IAW Congress in Helsinki preceded by workshop on 'Employment Patterns in the Eighties'. CSW accepted as affiliate of IAW. IHA member attends UN Conference on Disarmament in New York as observer for IAW.

1983 IHA asks government to apply for place on the UN Commission on the Status of Women. IHA hosts twelve members of the Deutscher Frauenring from Kronberg. IHA member presents paper to IAW Workshop in Cyprus on 'The Impact of Technology on Women in Employment'. Two members attend IAW Board meeting in London. IHA represented at Caradas, to promote responsible attitude to drink.

1984 IHA asks government to sign UN Convention on Elimination of Discrimination against Women. IHA member accompanies IAW president and vice-presidents to China at invitation of the All China Women's federation.

1985 UN Conference for End of Women's Decade in Nairobi attended by IHA Member as observer for IAW. Seven IHA members visit Deutscher Frauenring in Kronberg. IHA delegate attends IAW Workshop in Berlin on 'Sexism, Language and Education'.

1986 National Prices Commission disbanded by Minister. IHA organises public meeting on 'Use and abuse of Hormones and Antibiotics in Meat'. IHA delegate attends IAW Congress in Mauritius. IAW holds Peace Workshop for European Region in Bellinter Conference Centre, Navan, IHA and CSW help to organise it. IHA member invited to speak at Veterinary Congress in Galway on 'The Consumer's Right to Pure Wholesome Food'. IHA makes submission to the Advertising Standards Authority on the section of code applying to children.

1987 IHA monitors advertising practices and contact Director of Consumer Affairs and Fair Trading for information. IHA approaches National Association for Community Broadcasting with a view to broadcasting subjects of interest to women. Third Interdisciplinary Congress on Women held in Trinity College, Dublin. IHA members attend and help at information desk. IHA member attends IAW board meeting in London.

1988 IHA holds two public meetings on 'Irradiation of Food' and 'Violence in Society'. IHA represented on Consumer standards Consultative committee. IHA joins in 'Active Age Week'. IHA protests against misleading information on bank visa cards re holiday insurance. IHA against abortion but believes information should be available. IHA group visits European Parliament in Strasbourg.

1989 Visit of IAW president, Olive Bloomer. IHA delegate attends IAW Congress in Melbourne. Letter to government.

1990 IHA holds public meeting on 'The Consumer in the EC in 1992'. IHA member supports 'Going for Green' campaign and presses for elimination of CFCs and other pollutants. IHA writes to Taoiseach on his failure to appoint women to represent the government on the Economic and social commission.

1991 IHA makes submission to Second Commission on Status of Women on education for life; women in the home; unemployment and its effect on families; social welfare and responsibilities of deserting husbands and fathers.

1992 IHA celebrates Golden Jubilee and is busy preparing for the event. IHA calls for a new anti-litter campaign, involving teaching of civics and care of the environment in all schools. IHA hopes to be represented at IAW congress in Athens in September.

IHA Representation on Goverment and other bodies 1942-1992

1949 Buy Irish Committee; Andrée Skeffington. **1964** Lillie O'Callaghan

1959 Institute of Industrial Research and Standards; (Aluminium Sub-Com). Eileen Petrie; (Children's clothing) Hilda Tweedy.

1964 Women's Advisory Committee; Maude Rooney, Eileen Hackett, Doreen Johnston, Hilda Tweedy. **1971** Kay Daly, Sheila Kennedy, Maude Rooney, Eithne Moore.

1959 Prices Advisory Panel; Edith Cellem.

1967 Price Advisory Committee; Doreen Johnston.

1965 Youth Commission; Lillie O'Callaghan.

1965 Chemists Commission; Abigail Cassidy, Eileen Hackett.

1965 Dublin Council for the Aged; Kathleen Clarke, 1970 Muriel Hughes.

1966 Dublin Regional Committee; Muriel Hughes.

1966 National Council for Horticulture; Muriel Hughes.

1967 Canal Joint Committee; Rita O'Reilly

1967 Food Hygiene Advisory Committee; Kathleen Clarke.

1967 Rates Study Group; Maude Rooney.

1967 Community Consultative Council; Lilian Soiron, K McDonnell, 1971 Maureen Curran.

1971 Advisory Committee on the Metric System; Moira

Guiney, Jean Hollinshead.

1972 National Consumers Advisory Council; Betty Morrissey.

1972 Advisory Council on Transition to Value Added Tax; Moira Guiney, Gretta Morrison.

1972 National Prices Commission; Mairéad Allen.

1972 National Savings Committee; Sheila Kennedy.

1977 Consumer Education Committee; Maura O'Rourke.

1977 National Food Quality Assurance; Patrica Davys.

1977 National Federation of Drapers and Allied Traders Joint Footwear Sub-Committee; Connie Merriman.

1983 National Fruit and Vegetable Federation (ACOT); Moira Guiney.

1983 Federation of Urban and Rural Associations; Moira Guiney, Sheila Kennedy.

1983 COFACE Committee Exchange Information and Experiences between Family Organisations; Nora Browne, Gretta Morrison.

1983 Dublin City Council - Keep Dublin Tidy Committee; Abigail Cassidy.

1984 Caradas; Mairéad Allen, Moira Guiney.

1989 Keep Sunday Special Campaign; Ciarin Doherty.

1990 Consumer Standards Consultative Committee; Moira Guiney, Ciarin Doherty.

Brief bibliography

Ad Hoc Committee on Status of Women Minutes. Unpublished, 1968-1972.

Commission on the Status of Women, *Report to Minister of Finance*. Government Stationary Office, Dublin, 1972.

Cullen Owens, Rosemary, *Smashing Times*. Attic Press, Dublin, 1984.

Irish Housewives Association, *The Irish Housewife*. IHA, Dublin, 1946-1967.

Irish Housewives Association, *Housewives Voice*. IHA, Dublin, 1946-1967.

Irish Housewives Association, *Annual Reports and Papers*. IHA, Dublin, 1942-1992.

Levine, June, *Sisters*. Ward River Press, Dublin, 1982.

Mulvihill, Margaret, *Charlotte Despard: A Biography*. Pandora Press, London, 1989.

Sheehy Skeffington, Andrée, *Skeff*. Liliput Press, Dublin, 1991.

Whittick, Arnold, *Woman into Citizen*. Athenaeum, with Frederick Muller, London, 1979.

Index

138

141